Journey to Somewhere

One woman's quest for survival —
God's plan for sanctification

Melissa Amaya

This book is dedicated to all the

A Candle in the Window
Hospitality Network

families that welcomed me as a stranger.
(Matthew 25:35)

Contents

Part Three - Delighting in the Lord

Introduction

Four sweet kids bounce excitedly in their seats as I soberly jam the last of our bags into the car. I'm not nearly as excited. It's not that we have never taken a trip before, but this one is different. This time we won't be returning. Forced to leave our apartment, the previous seven days have been spent sorting through our belongings, picking out what will come and what will be left behind knowing that whatever is left will be chucked. No, this is unlike any road trip we have ever taken. This one is filled with uncertainty. Fear grips me as I settle into the driver's seat. With our most treasured belongings filling every square inch of our car we head off with a vague plan and no ultimate destination. All I have is my faith and my four children.

I never planned life this way; no one ever would. But here we are; all of our earthly possessions occupying the interior of a Toyota Highlander. It's not the first time we have moved and it's not the first time we have been h o m e l e s s. I shudder at the sound of that word. Homeless. I still can't bring myself to speak that word out loud. It is hard enough to type. Homeless. Without a home. No place to live. But it can't be. We don't look like homeless people are supposed to look. And besides, life wasn't meant to go this way. I'm a college grad. An Ivy League grad. I'm supposed to be enjoying the good life. A big house, a dog and a white picket fence, vacations to exotic locations and the newest car. That's *supposed* to be my story.

Instead, we are embarking on a homeless journey across the country as I figure out what to do next; a journey disguised as a year of homeschooling on the road. After all, what homeschooler hasn't dreamt about taking an epic road trip? I've dreamt about it too but in my dream it was planned and intentional, not frantic and by default because there was no other option. But I'm too stubborn and too determined to give in. I'm unwilling to let popular opinion determine my path or allow convenience to be the deciding factor for what is best for these children entrusted to me by God.

So I turn to the kindness of strangers, yet family. People I have never met, yet we are knit together as part of God's family. Through old fashioned, Christian hospitality we venture out with little but faith that our God will provide.

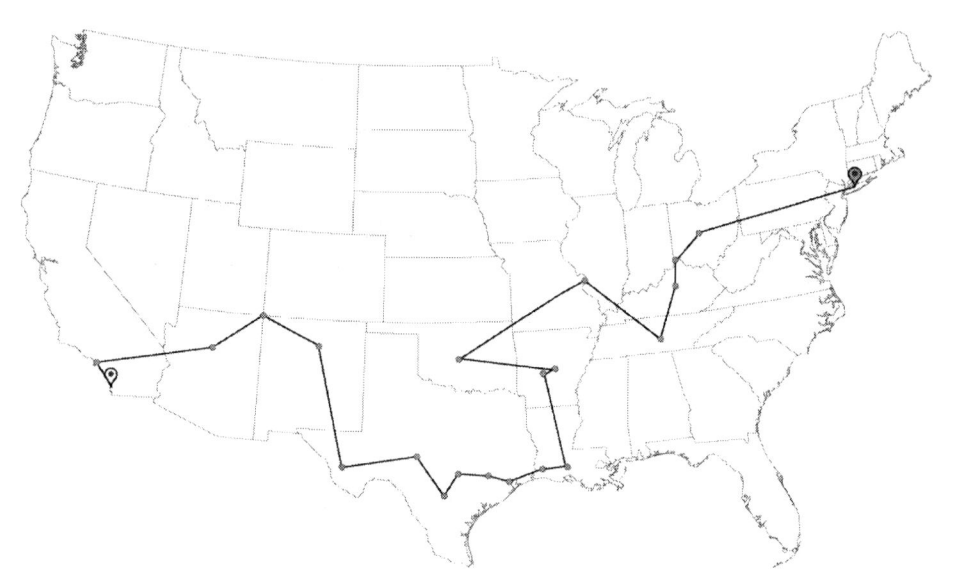

Part One

Fumbling in the Dark

A Late Arrival, an Early Departure

March 6

Pennsylvania. I know we are headed to Pennsylvania. Other than a name and an address, that's all I know. Part of my preparation over the past seven days has included numerous emails to complete strangers via a Christian hospitality website. In God's perfect timing and before I was aware that this trip would take place, I heard about the group: Christian families across the country that open their homes to other Christians who are traveling. It is because of this group of people that we have a place to go – rather places to go. Places to stay while we aimlessly roam. We are indeed transient, but will thankfully have a roof over our heads each night and food in our bellies.

Now, despite having the address plugged into the map on my phone I still manage to get lost, more than once. It's getting late and I am getting irritable. Actually, I've been irritable all day. The weight of the situation is unknown to my children, but I know. How sweetly they simply trust. They trust that Mom is in control and knows what she is doing. They wouldn't think to question whether there was a plan, but I know the reality; I am totally winging it. I might have a few homes lined up for overnight stays, but this is a plan-as-you-go endeavor with no end in sight. If only I could trust my Heavenly Father as much as these children trust their earthly mother.

*****

When we finally make it to our destination it is well after 9 pm. I did not plan on such a late arrival, but with my honed navigation skills I have a way of making a five-hour drive turn into nine. Despite the lateness and likely inconvenience the Pierre's greet us with warm smiles and helping hands to lug in our bags. I know I need to work out a better packing system. If we are going to make frequent stop-overs then I need a better way to pack our overnight necessities so that they will be easy to access. But that will have to wait. For now I have 4 tired children and one overwhelmed mama to get to bed.

After we each chug down a good bit of water we head off to the bedroom where we will be sleeping; the bedroom of the eldest daughter who is graciously giving up her very comfy room to complete strangers. There is a large bed, which the boys (2 and 4) and I will sleep in, and a mat with sleeping bags for my two girls. Partly due to the time, partly due to my shyness and largely due to the feeling of being a big stinking inconvenience and an imposition there is no small talk tonight. Not much more than "hello", "welcome", "thanks for having us", and "goodnight" are exchanged between our evening hosts and us.

*****

Morning arrives and I want out as fast as possible. It's all too much. The discomfort of reaching out to strangers, the discomfort of staying in their home topped off with the angst and uncertainty of the future. I want away from these people as fast as possible and before they see any hint of the inner turmoil I am experiencing. The only thing worse than taking this insane trip would be for someone else to chime in on the insanity. All Cynthia Pierre knows is that we are at the start of a homeschool road trip, and that is all she needs to know. The sooner we leave, the better the chances of maintaining my cover.

But alas, my plan for a quick departure is foiled by the four hungry bellies in my traveling party – all of whom express a hearty cheer to the question, "Are you sure I can't feed the children before you take off?" It seems easier to say, "Alright", easier to acquiesce to the kids' hunger than to awkwardly pack up the already jam packed car and get four hungry kids back into their seats. So we sit down to bagels and yogurt. Well, the kids do at least. My stomach has one too many knots to even think about food, but Cynthia insists that we be sent off with some pastries to enjoy later in the day.

We finally make our escape; I mean we say goodbye and head out. As we go, I can't help but reflect; I know what the Bible says about hospitality and I've read accounts of believers receiving other believers into their homes in the Scripture, but I have never seen that in action, at least not to this degree. These folks welcomed in a stranger with four young kids, expecting nothing from us but rather blessing us with warm beds at night and breakfast in the morning. Who are these people that take the command to show hospitality to strangers so literally and seriously?

So many more thoughts fly through my mind as we head west through Pennsylvania. Thoughts of uncertainty like, "What is the Lord doing?" "I need to line up more house stays come Tuesday", "Well, we survived and didn't end up dead in our beds," and the slightly less cynical "There are believers out there who are actively practicing hospitality. I can't wait to meet more of *these people*."

These people, because they seem a subset of the wider Christian community. *These people*, because they don't speak of hospitality in abstract terms with no intention of following through. They are living hospitable lives by opening their homes not only to friends but also to strangers. I would quickly learn that *these people* are indeed quite amazing and genuine. They are not seeking to earn praise from God or from man for their kindness, but rather from the heart ARE hospitable. It's not just something they do; it is who they are.

Stomach Bugs and Being Flexible

March 7

Not quite the exchange I was expecting on our second day in. It was hard enough to email Marsha a week ago to ask if we could stay, but now I have to call this stranger and *speak* to her on the phone? I think I might have a heart attack!

Not that I should be nervous. This is the same woman who just last week asked via email what kinds of meals we might like during our two day stay with her family and the same woman who reassured me of the heart of this network after I expressed great discomfort at requesting meals. I had grown so eager to meet this sweet woman in person and now it was clear she had forgotten.

After fifteen minutes of deliberation it seems there is nothing I can do but pull over and ring her number.

Me: "Hi Marsha. It's Melissa from the network. You asked me to call you."

Marsha: "Hi Melissa. I am so sorry. Each of our 8 kids fell sick one by one this past week with a stomach bug and your stay fell off our radar. I could quarantine a room for you guys if you'd like, but I'm not so sure you want to run the risk of catching what we've got. Traveling with a stomach bug is not too fun and this one is hanging around for a full week. It's your call."

Me: "Don't worry about it. You can't control sickness. We'll just stay in a hotel."

Marsha: "Then please let us pay for your hotel."

Me: "I can't do that."

Marsha: "Sure you can. You did everything right. You emailed us with plenty of notice, but we dropped the ball. My husband and I have already talked about it and we will take it out of our hospitality fund. There are two days of lodging and two days of meals that you were counting on receiving from us."

Me: "Um, okay," I mutter across the phone line as I say to myself, "I have never before met anyone that had a designated *hospitality fund*. Who budgets that?"

*Now, pride would ordinarily prevent me from accepting. 'I don't need help from anyone,' is my default position. I was raised to be self-reliant; even feminist to a degree. I am my own island and I can succeed on my own. That is what the world has taught me, but the Lord had another lesson for me to learn over the past three years of our current trial - accept the kindness of others when offered. Simply say 'thank you' and receive it as **His** kindness and provision for me rather than proudly and self-righteously say "no'"and thus deny the intended giver from the blessing of giving. It has been a hard lesson to learn for someone who grew up being taught the opposite.*

So the kids and I head to the local restaurant that Marsha recommended where we will grab dinner and where she will meet up with us. She arrives just as our food comes and we chat for a few minutes. This chat leaves me all the more sad that we will not have an extended visit with her family. Before she leaves, she hands me an envelope containing more than enough cash to cover our lodging and food for the next two days. What a blessing! What an amazing couple. What an amazing network of people.

Delayed Dinners and Sweet Fellowship

March 9

We are about to head off to the Boyd house for the night. The previous two days have been spent as tourists in the nearby area, buying time until today. With a schedule like ours there is no benefit to traveling fast. Everything about our travels is about buying time. I line up stays through the hospitality network for a night or two at a time. Once a stay is confirmed, there is no sense in bypassing that family - to do so would throw off the timing of the other homes already lined up and force me to find new places to stay on very short notice. So while we could have moved on from the area after the last home fell through it would not have been a benefit to do so. Instead, we lingered and had two fairly relaxing days before heading on to the next family.

It's Sunday, but we skipped church - I just didn't feel like "being on", answering the inevitable questions and comments: "Where are you from?", "Where are you headed?", and my personal favorite, "You're traveling without your husband? You are so brave."

We found a park in the afternoon so I could rearrange our packing system while the kids were happily occupied. We still need a better system. It is entirely too embarrassing to have a family watch my kids as they climb over and sit on top of various items in our over-flowing car and watch me as I smoosh, smash and jam the bags back into place. Oh, what I'd give for a quick dismount from the vehicle when we arrive at a home and an even quicker re-entry when we are leaving.

I just checked my watch - it's past time to go. For me I'm not on time unless I'm fifteen minutes early, and I especially loathe being late if someone is expecting me at a certain time. It's a respect thing. To be late is to say I value my time more than your time. It's a pet peeve of mine that has toned down somewhat in recent years, but punctuality is still a priority. So we need to get going if we're going to be on time. It's an hour drive from here and they are expecting us for dinner. I call out to the kids and they come barreling from the park and into the slightly more organized car.

We arrive at their street right on time, or at least what I think is their street. We drive up and down three times as my girls and I try and try to find their house number. "207 is on this side, Mom", Anna-bella calls out, "we're looking for 217" I reply, a little frazzled. Finally accepting the reality that another phone call is necessary and unavoidable I pick up my phone and dial their number.

Me: "Um, hi. This is Melissa from the network. I'm on your street but cannot find your house. The street seems to skip numbers."

Mrs B: "There's only 3 or 4 houses on our street. Are you sure you are on the right street?"

Me: "I think so. 217 Johnson Street, right?"

Mrs B: "That's the right address but something isn't right. Are you..."

Me: "Oh wait, my phone mapped me to the wrong city. I can't believe it. I'm so sorry. I'll be there in an hour."

Ugh. What a moron. I cannot stand being late yet I also have the amazing gift of getting lost - divine humor, I'm sure. We actually drove past their town after we left the park and could have been there an hour ago - what a waste of time, gas and miles on the car, not to mention a humbling first impression. I mean how many guests have they hosted that drove to the wrong *city*!?

We zip to the correct street as fast as possible and find their house without any trouble. As soon as we pull into the driveway we are greeted by Mr. Boyd and one of his sons, both of whom eagerly help gather our bags. My new and improved (yet still in process) packing system consists of 3 different pillow cases containing clothes (one for jammies, one for tomorrow's clothes and one for dirty laundry) as well as a toiletry bag.

As we enter the home, the entire family is waiting in the kitchen; quite a sight as they are a family of 12. Then it hits me - they were ready to eat an hour ago. The crockpots are all lined up, prepared to feed their family and mine, 17 people in total. They all wait patient-ly and politely (and I'm sure very hungrily) as small talk ensues before Mr. Boyd says "Let's eat."

A room full of grumbling kids would have seemed more "normal" after the extra delay while their idiot guests got the right address. Instead, not only did they wait but they also honored us by insisting that we go through the buffet line first. As we eat, I see that my kids seem to feel right at home. They seem as comfortable here as they would at a table of friends back in New York. How easily they adapt with each new situation! I, on the other hand, am still apprehensive about constantly meeting new people and staying in new homes.

My original plan to retire early and thus avoid the discomfort of socializing changes in an instant when I see the delight on Abigail's face. After dinner ends and before I can blink my 8 year old finds her way to a piano bench and is getting her first ever piano lesson. She has wanted lessons for almost two years but that was never in the realm of possibility - now in the home of strangers, on a trip I never wanted to take, she is getting her wish. I can't possibly take that from her just because her mother is an introverted fuddy duddy.

I stand around awkwardly for a few minutes before walking past the piano where Abigail is learning to play "Jesus Loves Me" and into the sitting room where the rest of the family has gathered. It seems the nightly routine is to gather here after dinner.

Without a word, each corner of the room is occupied as groups and teams form to engage over a plethora of board games. Backgammon over there. Parcheesi over here. Their youngest son, maybe 9 years old, has brought out his car collection and is engaging my 4-year old son in car play. Mrs. Boyd is sitting patiently as she tries to teach Annabella, my 6 year old, mancala. I look on, hoping Annabella understands the rules because I have no clue.

My fear of a dreadful night turns out to be unfounded as we enjoy a sweet time of fellowship. The night is capped off after Mr. Boyd gives everyone a five minute warning to finish up their games and gather for family worship. I must confess, it is a breath of fresh air to participate in family worship and not be the one leading. To sit back, watch a father lead his family, and simply follow along as my children and I are fed is spectacular. What a blessing to my own soul and to that of my children.

Looking Up

"The heavens declare the glory of God, and the sky above proclaims his handiwork. Psalm 19:1"

March 10

We rise before the sun today - long before the majority of the family. As quickly and as quietly as possible I shower, get everyone dressed and gather our things. We are headed to the Creation Museum today and I'm hoping to get there when the gates open. This will be our second time visiting the museum. The last visit was two years ago after a shorter road trip that kept us out of a homeless shelter. This time we have free passes, thanks to Mrs. Boyd, who is allowing us to borrow them -- another kindness from a stranger. At the bottom of the stairs we are greeted by the three oldest daughters who see us off with homemade muffins to enjoy later.

The excitement of free passes quickly wears off as the reality of life once again settles in. I am tired, so very tired. A physical exhaustion combined with emotional exhaustion mixed together with despair. Not an hour has gone by since we left New York five days ago that I have not worried about what we are doing and where we were going and how this would all turn out. But as we explore the museum I am reminded of God's sovereignty in all things.

*****

The kids bounce in line as we wait for our showtime at the planetarium (a perk of those free passes from the Boyd's). As the line starts moving forward, a sweet older man collects our tickets and gives us a warm smile as he greets each of the four faces with me. I feign a smile in return, hoping to disguise my utter exhaustion and hide the truth that I feel completely overwhelmed. "Hello" I say weakly as we walk past him and through the doors into the auditorium. Lagging behind the boundless energy in front of me I make my way down the aisle and fall back into my seat. Ah, it feels good to sit and I contemplate taking a wee nap while I have the chance.

 Soon the lights dim and we all recline in our seats to better see the "sky" above us. I start to close my eyes just as a booming voice jars me awake, narrating my virtual flight into the solar system.

"And God said, Let there be lights in the firmament of the heaven to divide the day from the night; and let them be for signs, and for seasons, and for days, and years:

And let them be for lights in the firmament of the heaven to give light upon the earth: and it was so.

And God made two great lights; the greater light to rule the day, and the lesser light to rule the night: he made the stars also.

And God set them in the firmament of the heaven to give light upon the earth,

And to rule over the day and over the night, and to divide the light from the darkness: and God saw that it was good. And the evening and the morning were the fourth day."

I listen and wonder, how did I never see this before? I have read the first chapter of Genesis many times. I am very familiar with the account of creation, but why have I never notice this before today?

By the power of His Word, God created all things. "He made the two great lights and *made the stars also*." **Also** - almost like an afterthought. How often have you, how often have I, stood outside and marveled at the stars in the sky? They are amazing. Sitting in this planetarium as we fly through space, through the Milky Way all the way to the outermost parts of the known universe, I can't help but marvel at my Creator. But what I glance up at, the stars that cause me to marvel at His creative hand, were created *also*. Side note. After thought.

Psalm 19:1 tells us, "The heavens declare the glory of God, and the sky above proclaims His handiwork."

In the midst of my exhaustion, I sit in the theater in a daze. My God is so big! He made all of this. He knows every square inch of His creation, yet He also made man. "What is man that You are mindful of him, and the son of man that You care for him?" Psalm 8:4. God made the sun and the moon, the stars also. He made stars beyond what we can even see. Yet, He also made us and knows each of us intimately. He formed every aspect of our being and He cares.

I sit here in my distress and remember that God cares. And He is in control. Every detail of my life, including the current circumstance, are neither beyond His control nor beyond His care. In fact, He orchestrated this very trial for my good! Romans 8:28 reminds me of this truth: "And we know that for those who love God all things work together for good, for those who are called according to His purpose." He knows and He cares and He is orchestrating it all to make me more like Christ.

The show ends, I stagger to my feet and walk out of the theater humbled. In light of the universe, I do not even show up as a speck. I am such a minuscule part of His creation, without any intrinsic value of my own. And yet He has chosen to lavish His love upon even me in that while I was yet a sinner, Christ died for me (Romans 5:8). For a brief moment I feel a reprieve from the stress. Circum-stances haven't changed, a solution didn't present itself, but I have, ever so slightly, as I remember who my God is, what He has already done and what He has promised to do.

Crochet and Play

March 11, 12, 13

I don't like to bother people. It's an unofficial rule I try to live by -- don't bother others. It's the second rule right after don't be late, although in a true poll they may indeed tie for first place. Don't bother others. Don't impose upon them. Don't get in their way. Don't inconvenience them. As a parent, I also don't want my kids to bother others. Now, I'm not claiming that any of this is a healthy way to live, but it is the way I am. So when my children are in a position where they interact with adults I'm usually thinking, "please don't bother them, please don't talk too much or ask too many questions or otherwise be a bother." Take that mentality and apply it to my aversion of meeting new people and my brain is bound to overload.

It's rather cold when we arrive at the next house. I'm glad we still have our winter coats handy. The sky looks like it might actually snow. We pull up to the curb in front of the house - a house that literally has candles in each window. "How quaint" I think to myself.

We are met by a warm smile at the door and walk into a home that is precisely decorated and immaculately clean. All I can think at the sight is, "I hope my kids don't cause trouble and don't make a mess." Visions of dirt tracked across the carpet and broken things falling off of shelves flash through my mind.

Not that my kids are troublemakers -- they are usually good kids. And not that they have a habit of trashing places, but they are kids and do spill from time to time. The family certainly did nothing to make me feel unwelcome or put me on edge. They knew we were coming and that "we" included four young kids, so they weren't surprised by the five people standing at their door. They were welcoming and kind and gracious - yet those were indeed my first thoughts.

*****

I desire for my girls to learn the lost arts that all women used to know and I am grateful that they are not only willing to learn them but also eager. Unfortunately I have no ability to pass those skills on - I was never taught the art of sewing or crocheting or knitting. I was never even taught how to cook - that I figured out on my own after I left home. So it is an utter delight to see my sweet girls take an interest in these skills and today both my girls will check off "first crochet lesson" right under "first piano lesson".

The Moore family consists of dad, mom, and two teenage girls. The girls are just as sweet as their mother with beautiful smiles and even more beautiful spirits. Accomplished musicians as well as avid crocheters they eagerly offer a round of piano lessons to my girls during our stay as well as instruction on the basics of crochet. The Moore's are truly a fun and joyful family and watching them interact is a refreshing escape from the turmoil constantly going on in my own heart and mind.

After breakfast today we attempt to explore the area while the family goes about their daily routine. I say "attempt" because it is so bitterly cold and windy that the outdoor sites I had planned are unbearable. So long before noon I realize plan A is out the window. With a whole day to fill and not much motivation or energy I opt for the easy route and find the local movie theater.

We don't watch many movies. I am very aware that everything my children (and I for that matter) are exposed to will influence them either towards God or away from God and more and more movies these days do the latter. However, a movie can indeed offer me a respite so I do occasionally take the easy way out for the sake of quiet -- now is one of those times. The thought of sitting and relax-ing for a whole hour and twenty-three minutes is very appealing and so we head into the theater hoping there is an acceptable option.

Mr. Peabody. My kids recognize him immediately from the old Rocky and Bullwinkle cartoon I introduced them to via Netflix. How bad could Peabody be? Hesitantly, I buy our tickets and settle in for the show. A few laughs later the show ends and thankfully I'm not aghast.

Actually, we are left with a half-decent take-away: Sherman (the boy) should trust Mr. Peabody's (the dog) motives and not assume something good is being kept from him because Peabody has always proved himself faithful and trustworthy. (if the boy-dog thing confuses you, find Rocky and Bullwinkle reruns). What a good lesson for my kids to learn – to trust me even when they don't understand. Actually, what a great reminder for me: I can continue to trust God because He has always proved Himself faithful and trustworthy.

In the morning, we head to rural Tennessee; a stop unnecessary as far as a logical route goes, but it will buy us another night and the network profile of this family is sure intriguing. It's a home without any young kids so despite wanting to meet them I am once again nervous.

Homes with young kids feel more comfortable. The parents are in a similar season of life; they are in the thick of child training and surely have kids who do not always behave as well as mom and dad would like. Homes with kids are usually child friendly, containing toys and maybe even a less than perfectly clean house. But if the children are older or out of the home all together, I can't help but wonder, "Do they remember what having kids is like?" "Will they be patient with the ways of kids - the goofiness, even foolishness, the child's sense of humor and topics of interest?" Or "will my children be a bother and an annoyance to them?"

But while these are my instinctual thoughts, the truth is that I don't need to place a burden on my children that does not belong to them. It is neither helpful nor right to blame them for the behavior of others. My kids are taught that they are responsible for their own behavior *and* their own responses to the *behavior* of others. Alexander, my five-year-old, cannot blame his anger on what his sister did – he needs to own it. If I hold that standard within our family why would I fault my child for the misbehavior of others outside of our family? Why would I place a guilt on them that does not belong to them? If someone chooses annoyance in response to my children being children it is not my problem, nor my children's. I should and can leave it at that.

I know all of that in my brain, yet the fear of man rears its ugly head as we arrive at this home of mom, dad and two adult daughters. The fear, however, quickly fades. Cathy Perez greets us warmly and asks an unexpected question: "do the kids need to get some energy out in the yard?"

This question isn't her attempt to get rid of them; she comes outside too, as do her two daughters. Rather it is her attempt to meet their needs, recognizing that after a day of driving the kids might want to run around.

Sarah and Courtney, who surpass the age of my kids by a decade or two, don't hesitate to lead a parade of kids waving streamers. Instead of disinterested adults who give the requisite greetings and then retreat to "more important things" they eagerly and excitedly join my children in play.

I eventually get cold and convince my children that they also want to come back inside. We sit down on comfy couches and I notice how child friendly the house appears. I suspect it's partly their no frills, down home decorating style, which is absent of little knickknacks and trinkets, but wonder how much is intentional. When I comment on the unique flooring Cathy informs me that it's made of reclaimed barn wood, "good for kids" she says without missing a beat, "no one will ever notice a scratch or dent in this floor".

There has been a common thread in each of the families we have stayed with so far – older children have not hesitated to include and engage the younger ones. And it hasn't appeared to be out of duty or obligation because mom gave them a pep talk ahead of time reminding them to be kind. It's been a strange, genuine, from the heart desire to interact with the youngins, just as they would with someone closer in age. There has been no invisible barrier preventing a 13-year-old, or in this case, a 31-year-old, from engaging with my 2, 4, 6 and 8 year olds.

David soon returns from work as Sarah and Courtney tag-team dinner preparations.

Mealtime in other homes is another layer of stress. What embarrassing thing might one of my children say or do? How poorly will their already poor table manners be on display? Will they spill or make a mess? And will any of it bother our host?

Maybe one day I won't care so much what others think - I can only
imagine how freeing that might be. But on this day, as we sit down
to a wonderfully kid-friendly dinner, I am far from free. Analyzing
each child's every move, I internally cringe as one speaks with a
bread stick rolling around her mouth, and as another picks up the
noodles with his hands, completely ignoring the perfectly good fork
laying next to his plate. "What are they thinking?" "Do they think
I'm a horrible mother because my children eat with their hands and
talk with food in their mouths and don't sit perfectly still?" Not one
of the Perez' *looks* bothered by my kids, but maybe they are just
pretending.

Dinner ends without any big disaster and my kids retreat once again
to the play loft, joined by Sarah while I help clean up. The children
still don't seem to have any trouble adjusting from home to home.
They embrace the invitation to "make yourself at home" even before
it is verbalized. I envy their ability to not worry about what others
think. They are who they are and don't seem to wonder if who they
are is acceptable to others. As their mom it is, of course, my job to
mold and shape them and to teach them proper manners and eti-
quette, but my children don't get stuck on formality. They have
embraced each new person as they would an old friend. It's amazing.

With Sarah monitoring the kids playing in the loft overhead, Cathy,
David, Courtney and I sit and talk. We speak of theology and family.
How and why they moved from California to rural Tennessee and of
life in general. All too quickly it is long past bedtime so I politely
state that I need to get my kids to sleep. David asks if we have a few
more moments as they always do Bible reading as a family before
bed and would we like to join them? Just like at the Boyd's house
the answer is an emphatic yes. My kids will see the priority of
Scripture reading from someone other than me, they will see a man,
a father leading his family – quite possibly the only time they will
see that is with other families – and I will receive some soul feeding.

So one by one the kids pile down the ladder from the loft area. We
all grab our Bibles and get comfortable on the couches as David
opens the Word. It's clear he has adjusted their normal study, both in
length and in depth, to accommodate the little people listening. How

very thoughtful. It's also clear that his priority isn't to create an aura of superiority by showing how much more knowledgeable he is than we are, but rather to minister to the souls in the room – specifically the little souls still in need of a changed heart. He doesn't dumb down the Bible, nor does he pull out a "Children's Bible". No, he keeps to the Scriptures, but has his audience in mind. He keeps the reading shorter for their sake and expounds at a level that they can understand.

Ah, how refreshing. Honey to my soul to hear the Word read and explained rightly. And so relaxing to know my children are being fed at the same time as me – and I'm not doing the feeding. I'll be quite honest, I'm exhausted most of the time, and the weight of shepherding my children alone, teaching them God's Word and daily showing them their need for a Savior -- filling the role my husband *should* be filling -- is daunting and exhausting. It is a relief to have them hear Scripture read and explained by someone other than me. It is an encouragement to see families functioning rightly, with mom and dad each filling their God-given roles. And I can only hope that it is an encouragement to my kids to see a dad leading his family. I pray it impresses on their minds the way it *should* be so that my boys aspire to be that kind of man and my girls aspire to marry that kind of man.

Bible time ends and we get washed up for the night. After I tuck in the kids I settle myself into bed and stare at the ceiling. This is the third family we have eaten supper and spent an evening with - and the third family that managed to interact with each other absent of media -- no television to drown out the boredom, as there was no boredom. These families actually talked to each other. They pulled out board games and played with each other. No one needed a cell phone or a tablet. I didn't see pockets of isolation as children or parents entered their own private worlds of personal media.

It was not uncommon for someone to randomly jump on the piano (all three families had one) to play a tune or two. It was wonderful and refreshing and hopefully made an impression on my crew of little people who would choose to spend their days with their brains falling out in front of a television if given the option. It gives hope to me that families truly can function without media being a crutch and children can be happy even without the latest episode of some show.

Now, I don't know that any of these families would call media a sin. Maybe they would; I know I don't. For me, it is not about drawing a hard and fast rule that says TV is of the devil, but my vision for my children is that they would find their joy not in media but in Christ. And they would be able to *create* their own fun and entertainment and not rely on a screen to entertain them.

I saw cell phones in more than one of these homes, but no one was tied to that phone. They didn't obsessively check their email or their Facebook account (not that I've ever had that problem). They were able to put it down and function without it and turn to the other people in their home for relationship.

*****

After breakfast the next morning I find myself lingering much longer than originally planned. Along with a desire to not bother people goes a fear of overstaying my welcome. I'm sure I over think it (I over think most things), but what is the balance between not rushing out after breakfast and appearing rude versus staying too long after breakfast and overstaying a welcome? I'm sure the line is some-where, but for now I am enjoying the conversation with Sarah, Courtney and Cathy and really don't want to leave. Thankfully, our drive today is only a few hours so when we do finally leave, a few hours later than expected, no harm is done.

Stomach Bugs, Flat Tires and First Impressions

March 14

There is only one chance to make a first impression and this was hardly the impression I hoped to give.

We arrive on a Friday to find five kids playing outdoors - kids with ages similar to my own. It's a refreshing sight and I know I'll be able to relax a bit. Unless their kids are some alien mutants these folks are used to kid things - their energy, their enthusiasm, their less than perfect behavior at times. I'm very much looking forward to this stay.

Jon and Caroline Harvey are quick to greet us and my kids waste no time joining in the fun, including jumping on the trampoline which seems to be the main event outside. The Harvey's had prepared the apartment above the garage for us, but Caroline offers an alternative when she sees my kids. "I don't know why, but I thought you had teenagers and figured they would want more privacy than our full house can offer, but if you prefer to be in the main house with us we can do that." I politely decline telling her that she has already gone to the trouble of prepping the apartment, we'll be just fine there.

Now, that is 100% true, but it is also a relief to know we will have our own space. My introverted self is still adjusting to this constant travel and constant interaction with new people; space and time and quiet sound very nice.

The kids play together all afternoon, right up until dinner time. As we sit down to dinner, Jon and Caroline say that we are the first people to stay with them through the network. (I can't help but hope it's a positive experience for them.) By the time dinner ends, it's dark outside and nearly bedtime. We say goodnight and head out the back door, down the deck stairs, across the short gap between the house and garage and back up a set of stairs to get to the apartment. It's 7:30 pm by the time we wash up and all my kids are fast asleep not long after. Just as I begin to drift off to sleep a rumbling in my stomach startles me awake.

Oh, this is not hunger. No, this was the worst kind of rumbling. In short, I spend the next 7 hours rising in exactly 20 minute intervals. By 2 am, the violence has calmed and I lay in bed completely drained, physically weak and incredibly sore.

Morning comes and I can barely open my eyes. My head feels like cement against the pillow. Clearly the activity I had planned for us today would be postponed.

(Yesterday on our way to the Harvey house, we stopped at Stones River National Park – a Civil War battle site, now turned museum. They had begun to work on the Junior Ranger Badge, but time and impatience (mine) caused us to leave before they finished. This was our first exposure with the Junior Ranger program, which is aimed at encouraging youth to learn about our nation's history at each National Park and Historical Site. My girls had answered about half of the questions required in their booklets and the plan for today was to return to Stones River so they could finish earning the badge.)

"Abigail, give me 15 more minutes" turns into an hour. Eventually, the deadline I gave myself to get up and take a shower arrives. I swing my feet over the side of the bed, my head makes it two-inches above the pillow before I crash back down and admit defeat. "I'm sorry Abigail", I say to my oldest, "I just cannot get up yet, but I promise I will take my shower at 10 am and I will really try to take us to that park."

We hadn't traveled here to be stuck in a room, yet there is no way I can do anything. My girls get themselves dressed and somehow manage to get the boys dressed as well. The four of them head down the steps, across the grass, up the back steps to the house porch and into the kitchen to join the Harvey's for breakfast. I vaguely recall them leaving.

I don't like bothering people, yet now I would be a bother to these people I had met less than 24 hours before. Just great! I would have done anything to prevent being such a nuisance, but the Lord made sure I was completely incapable. I would have to rely on the kindness and hospitality of these strangers - I guess I should call them new friends, for they will act in the most loving ways possible.

My oldest dutifully returns after breakfast to give me an update. The other three are busy playing with their new friends and my instruction to come back after breakfast seems to have been forgotten. I give Abigail permission to go play as well. Since I am in no position to collect the other three it seems pointless and unfair to sequester her.

At 10 am, I rise as promised and take my shower. Rise might be too strong a word. It's more like I roll off the bed, somehow steady myself and drag my weary frame to the bathroom. Everything is in slow motion and what is normally a five minute process turns into 35. But I do it. There, I keep my word. I shower and now I a m r e t u r n i n g t o b e d.

I just cannot do anything. I am clean but still feel just as weak, just as sore, just as exhausted. I crash back on the bed and at some point offer apologies once again to Abigail when she returns to check on me – apologies that we would not be going anywhere today.

At 4 pm, I wake up to the sound of my 6 year old in the bathroom. "When did she get back? I never heard her come up the stairs," I wonder. But I certainly recognize the sounds coming from behind that door. Another one. Fantastic. Now Annabella is sick as well. We must be the absolute worst guests ever!

Whether it's my body recovering or the shock and embarrassment of another family member being ill in this home, I finally have enough strength to get up. I steady myself against the wall and slowly make my way down the stairs. Caroline Harvey has known us since only yesterday yet she has spent the whole day babysitting my children. In addition to how I feel physically I am also horribly embarrassed not only about being physically sick while in their home but also for imposing on them, quite unintentionally, to care for my kids for a full day.

When I finally make it outside Caroline is standing at the base of the stairs that lead to the upper porch. I make me way over to her and tell her I am not feeling well. "Yes, Abigail told me. I am so sorry you are sick." "I feel awful" I say about the imposition we have become. "You look awful" is the reply. With that I chuckle, "Ha, no. I *feel* physically awful, but I also feel awful that you've had to watch my kids all day." "Oh, please don't. They are fine. I don't mind watching them if you don't mind." Not that I can do anything about it anyway, but she seems sincere enough so I said thank you and head back to bed.

With a few more hours of sleep, I feel like a new woman. Still a little achy, but I can walk upright without feeling dizzy. It is rare for me to get sick and especially rare for me to get sick like this. But in times of illness, I am reminded of how very blessed I am that most of the time my body works like it was designed to work. I'm certain this is yet another way that the Lord is working on my pride and need for independence. But maybe it is also intended to stir up gratefulness in my heart; gratefulness that health is the norm in my life and that even in sickness my body works to restore itself back to health. God is amazing and His creation is amazing. We are indeed fearfully and wonderfully made.

I am well enough to head over for dinner. I'm not hungry and am a bit nervous about eating, still I know my body desperately needs nutritional replenishment after all that has transpired. So I mostly enjoy the fellowship and eat a little. I thank Caroline profusely for watching the kids and for doing what seems like endless loads of laundry for us. Who wants to wash the dirty laundry of a family they just met? But Caroline didn't bat an eye. Earlier in the day she insisted on giving us clean sheets and washing our dirty clothes stating, "I have kids too and laundry isn't a big deal." Maybe not a big deal for her, but it's a huge deal for me.

In the midst of my apologies, Caroline points out the obvious, "It's a blessing that you weren't on the road when the bug hit." Very true. And what a *coincidence* that not only did we just happen to stay with a family that has an apartment but also that Caroline misread our profile and prepped that apartment thinking my children were older. It could have been so much worse.

We could have been in their home instead of in the apartment – they could have endured the sound of every bathroom visit I took the night before. Or worse, we could have been driving and I could have been incapable of caring for them in a place where there was no one else to help.

But God in His kindness gave me a reprieve and offered a dose of humble pie at the same time. It is humbling to be at the mercy of others. Humbling to need help, let alone help from a stranger. The past three years have been a long lesson in humility and this bout of illness is part of the curriculum.

Our stay here is *supposed* to be two days, which means that we are *supposed* to be leaving in the morning. Jon told us to stay as long as we needed, that there is no rush at all. I am so glad he did because the fun isn't over yet.

Sunday

How wonderful a good night of sleep feels! I slept like a baby and despite lingering soreness I feel a bit better. Annabella is another story. While the other three cross over to the house for breakfast, I stay in bed with her while she sleeps.

It is funny how the Lord works, and rarely is it how we would choose. Just a few days earlier as I surveyed my progress with work I realized I needed a few focused days to catch up. By God's grace I have a job I can work remotely with very flexible hours. But with so much constant travel I've fallen behind on some record keeping and now I need to catch up before it gets worse.

In God's providence we are stuck for the day. We won't be doing any touristy activities as I'm still not 100% and neither is Annabella. So there isn't much to do other than rest, be here for Annabella when she wakes up and hop on my computer to work. Instead of spending money on a hotel for a few days to get the needed downtime we stay with the same wonderful people and my children play with their new friends. Thank you Lord for this stomach bug.

Will I be able to thank Him for what comes next?

Annabella eventually wakes up and is feeling a bit better. We walk outside together to get some fresh air, see sunlight and let everyone know we are still alive. As I survey the yard to see where everyone is my eye is drawn to the front right tire of my car. "Hmm, that looks funny. Did we run over a ball? That's all I need. First we get sick in their home now we popped a ball." The closer I get to the car the less it looks like a ball under the tire. "Oh no, I'd rather a popped ball."

Add a flat tire to the mix, that's all I need. First, I get sick then my daughter gets sick, necessitating a longer stay than expected, now I couldn't leave even if I wanted to. I must confess that my first thoughts are not praise and thanksgiving. That will come later.

I meander into the main house in a bit of a daze and all the more embarrassed by the amount of inconvenience I've created for this family. Much to my surprise they already know about the tire and Jon is already working on a solution.

During my short walk from the driveway into the house, I was planning out *my* solution. "I'm a AAA member, I'll call them and get a tow. I always get my tires at Costco - I know there is one about 15 miles away. AAA will only tow 3 miles so I have to figure something out..."

Being the self-sufficient, "modern" woman that I am I outline my solution to Jon who ever so graciously smiles and says he will call Costco, but it's obvious he has something else in mind. With an outright battle in my own mind I thank him and turn to find my kids.

Contradiction. Pure contradiction.

"I've got this!" I want to scream out, yet it's so nice to have someone else problem solving on my behalf. After being on my own for over two years – left to fend for myself for over two years - I am tired of making decisions. Flat out tired. So despite the initial urge to take charge I choose instead to rest and allow Jon to fix this for me. I humble myself (yet again) and allow the Lord to use this man as His hands and feet to care for my children and me.

A bit later in the day, after resting some more, I come down the apartment stairs to see Jon standing beside my car putting on a donut. His donut. To get to my spare would require a complete unpacking of the whole back of the car, but Jon has the same make of car and is instead using his own spare. I ask him again about Costco - I'm a loyal Costco shopper and am probably a bit insistent in my tone. He gently informs me that he did indeed call Costco but it was quite a bit more expensive than Discount Tires, who also does free rotations – just like Costco.

Alright then, "do you want me to give you cash or are you comfortable using my card. How do you want me to pay for this?"

"We've decided to take care of this for you. I don't know your situation, I don't want to know", he says with waving hands, "'but we are in a position where we can do this for you to bless you. And I want to make sure you have four new tires because I'm concerned that if we don't do that now you will end up with another flat later on in your trip."

With tears in my eyes I squeak out, "Thank you. That is a blessing, you have no idea how much of a blessing. Thank you so much!"

One of the many things the Lord has taught me over the past three years is instead of saying, "No, I'm okay" to say, "Thank you" and receive whatever the offer of help may be. Whether physically in carrying something, practically in watching my children or financially in giving $10 or $100. My pride wants to say, "No, I'm okay" but humility says something different.

Humility isn't weak and it isn't exaggerating a situation to seek pity. It is being willing to admit the reality of a situation. Humility says, "I'm tired and overwhelmed" when asked, "How are you?" instead of feigning strength.

Pride in this area also denies the *giver* the blessing of *giving*. God works differently than us. His ways are higher than ours and He is working out **all things** for His own glory. So there is glory when one of His children gives to aid another believer. There is glory when the recipient humbly accepts help. "This is how the world will know you are my disciples, that you love one another" (John 13:35). God wants to bless the giver, He wants to bless me by providing something I need and we ought to bless God by acting as His children.

Thank you, Jon Harvey. And ultimately thank you, Lord, for your kindness to me, a wretched sinner. You provide for all of my needs and often at the moment of need. Thank you, Lord.

Before the details of the tire fix were discussed, Jon had asked if we needed anything else. I mentioned that I wanted to find a roof top carrier as the rear carrier was a bit overloaded and I was worried about the strain it was putting on the car. He knew of a discount store where overstock items were sold and he would look there.

Jon would spend half of the day tomorrow, Monday, taking care of my car. Late in the day he returns with the tires replaced and a new roof top carrier. Not a discount carrier from the overstock store, but a top of the line, brand spanking new carrier. Jon and his son J.J. install the new carrier and ever so patiently load it, item-by-item, as I sorted through what is needed inside the car and what could be stashed away up there.

After car repacking we all sit down for dinner and my girls do what they aren't supposed to do. They spill the beans and inform Caroline that mommy's birthday is tomorrow. Begrudgingly, and probably red-faced, I endure 'Happy Birthday' from 9 kids and two adults. My birthdays aren't something I care much to celebrate. I'd be content to pass the day without any acknowledgement of its significance. I don't mind the getting older part; it's the remembrance of who won't be celebrating with us that hurts; the memory of broken dreams and deep hurts. But once beans are spilled, there is no undoing it.

In the morning we pack up. Jon and Caroline make it clear that we are welcome to stay as long as we need or want, and I believe them. But it is time to go. There is a fine line between a perfectly pleasant departure where both sides are wishing they had more time together and overstaying one's welcome where both sides know it's time to go. So with new wheels, new storage and an abundance of snacks that Jon bought for us (at Costco, no less) we pile in, wave goodbye and are on our way. I am so grateful for our time here, yet wonder if our stay may have ruined their enthusiasm for hospitality through this network. We were their first guests – will we be their last?

*****

On our way out of the area we stop back at Stones River National Park where my girls finish up their Junior Ranger badge. Smiling ear to ear, they both raise their right hand and recite the ranger code after the park ranger. With their newly pinned badges, the girls skip their way to the car like they just won the Olympics. I couldn't be prouder or happier to see them so gleeful.

It is indeed my birthday today, 33 years old. I'm glad the kids are excited about it solely because it means they haven't been completely desensitized to life. Despite all that they have endured in the last few years they still find joy in life. And quite honestly, if it wasn't for them -- for their enthusiasm and excitement for life -- I'd likely be a much more sullen person.

To make the day more special than usual we head to Lambert's Café. We don't need an excuse to hit up Lambert's. Anytime we are near one we find time to stop in, but it just so happens that today we have a legitimate excuse - birthday lunch.

If you've never been to a Lambert's let me try to explain: Cracker Barrel decor (cool old stuff hanging all over the walls), sturdy, rustic wood tables with paper towels that serve both as napkins and as plates. You order your (oversized) meal from the menu and then gorge yourself on the "pass arounds" as you wait:

- Fried okra
- macaroni and tomatoes
- fried potato and onion
- black eyed peas.

Servers walk around and pile the "pass arounds" on your paper towel. Delicious. One could easily fill up on the "pass arounds", and I usually do. Oh, and then there are rolls tossed at your head. After all they are the "Only Home of the Throwed Roll". They've been throwing rolls at people since 1942. The rolls alone are worth the visit, especially when topped with their sorghum or apple butter. And this is my kids' favorite part - it's the reason we visit Lambert's whenever it is on our route.

I was introduced to Lambert's in Sikeston, MO some 10 years ago, the same Lambert's we will visit today. A group of us from church went up from Mississippi for the day. It was a blast and the only thing missing for me was my husband, who had to work that Saturday. So when his birthday came just a few weeks later I knew what we would do. "Get in the car, I have a surprise for you" was all he knew as we drove the two hours so that he could experience the fun I had just a few weeks earlier.

Today, as we drive north on what is a very familiar road I have mixed emotions. A flood of memories from our trip there together and the sadness of the decline since then pierce my spirit as I try to rejoice in what is before me.

In this car are my four precious children, gifts from God. While the Lord saw fit to take one thing from me, it would be wrong to over-look the blessings He is giving to me, even in this moment. Never-theless, I can't help but think maybe if the kids called him right now and told him where we were going, maybe then it would prick his heart and he would remember the good times and the Holy Spirit would use that to convict him and bring my husband to repentance and a restored relationship with God and then with his family.

But I know better than to try to orchestrate my husband's repentance or choreograph the future. God doesn't need my help and He is working things behind the scenes so much bigger and grander than I can possibly imagine. He has said "no" to my repeated petition of a restored marriage, not out of vengeance, nor as a punishment, but out of love and a desire to give me something even better. My role is not to tell God how to do it but to submit to His plan and His **timing** as I wait upon Him.

Part of the better has already been given. Part of it is the trial itself and the blessings that only come through trials.

A closer fellowship with Him.

Countless times I have fallen asleep while crying over the pages of my Bible only to wake in the morning with prayers and petitions on my lips. That never happens when all is well.

Part of the blessing is the refinement I have gone through and am still undergoing. I am more like Jesus today than I was two years ago because He is showing me the secret idols of my heart, humbling me in my pride, revealing to me in the most tangible ways possible

His goodness, His provision, and that He is indeed all I need. He is enough, even in the darkest moments. He is enough, even when I feel lost and forsaken by friends and family. He is enough, even when I am flat out of strength, because it is when I am weak that I am strong. It is when I acknowledge I have no strength or power of my own that He chooses to show me His strength and power, enabling me to do what I have been called to do.

Oh yes, countless blessings, through raindrops and through tears. Through sleepless nights when I am keenly aware that He is all I have to cling to.

So as best I can I turn off the tears welling in my eyes and turn my heart to the Lord as these tears of sorrow are replaced by heartfelt gratitude for all that He has done for me. There is still a lingering sorrow. Still the thought of, "I wish he was here with us." But I cannot control the externals. I certainly cannot control him; I have learned that full well. All I can do is raise my hands to the One who gives and takes away, as He sees fit.

The hustle, bustle and entertainment of Lambert's is a welcome distraction. Just as soon as we are seated the kids are on the look out for the roll man and as soon as he is in sight their hands go up, indicating that they wanted a roll. *Whizzzzzz*, incoming! One by one they each put out their arms and try their best to catch. Most rolls end up on the floor. A few bounce off a body part - arm, chest, even face - before bouncing on the table or the bench. "Clean enough", I say, "5 second rule" and eyes light up as they slop on the butter. And every so often there is actually a clean catch. Well, mostly clean. It doesn't hit the ground or table or bench so despite a bit of bobbling it comes to stop in the arms of an incredibly excited child.

All in all the meal is a success. Bellies are full. Children are entertained. And I am rejoicing in God's kindness to me.

Arches, River Boats and Lewis & Clark

March 19

We arrive at Sandra's house with little difficulty, much to my surprise given my questionable navigation skills. As we pull over to park in this quaint neighborhood my kids manage to spot a park right down the street and are already making requests to go and play. "Maybe" is my pat response when a "no" would likely induce groaning and whining. A "maybe" is what they get.

Sandra is quick to meet us at the car and gives a most enthusiastic welcome. She ushers us into her house where we meet Brody, her adorable little pomadoranean. The kids are smitten. It seems any four footed creature yields a power over my children in which they become calm and gentle and start speaking in high pitched voices as they say, "aw, doggy".

Despite her jovial and laid back personality I feel uneasy as we enter her pristine home.

Dust free		2 year old boy
Organized	+	4 year old boy
Childless		6 year old girl
Precisely decorated		8 year old girl

NERVE WRACKING

She shows us the basement where we will be staying, an area just as nice as the upstairs. Of course my kids immediately zoom in on the hand weights and exercise balls. Before I have a chance to stop them all four are like flies on fruit as they begin testing their strength and bouncing like monkeys. Ms. Sandra kindly states that all of the exercise equipment is off limits for their own safety. My kids quickly comply, but will need a few more reminders before our stay is over.

As we sit down to dinner in the evening, my focus is on the four bouncing bodies. I am much more concerned about monitoring manners and messes than I am about my food. While I am glad my children seem to adjust so well and are quite comfortable regardless of whom they are around, I sometimes wish they were a bit more reserved. But that is really just a cop-out. It's just another way to say I wish they were more like me – as if the world needs four more of me.

The next day we wake to scrambled eggs and a smiling Sandra. She gives us some suggestions for things to do around the city and hands me a key. "I'll be delayed this afternoon with client meetings, and would you let Brody out when you got back?"

Departures from a house are always stressful. The embarrassment of how jam packed my car is makes a quick getaway desirable. Any extra moment we linger is a moment they might look into the car as the kids load up. Will she see the pile of items that form a wall? It takes some finesse to enter and exit without anything falling out the door, a finesse that has mostly eluded us.

Rare, posed picture. Cape Girardeau, MO

Departures are also a time when my kids are excited and getting all four into the car can be a feat. So it is a time when, at least in my head, my parenting skills are on display for critique. "Do her kids obey? Why aren't they listening faster? She said 'get in the car' five minutes ago, why is that one picking grass and the other one wrestling with his brother?" At least that is what I imagine people thinking.

Is that what I think when I watch other families load kids into a car?

Nope. Not unless it is met with outward defiance and the parent makes no attempt to parent. Otherwise I usually look and smile as I think about the energy level of children. So why do I hold others to a different standard? Why do I assume they would be any less gracious than I am when I know my own thoughts and just how sinful and selfish those thoughts can be? In a way I am assuming the worst about others, not to mention fearing the opinion of man. How wicked! God is my Father and to Him only do I answer for my parenting.

In my better moments I can turn an otherwise stressful load up into a fun and playful one by scooping up a wandering child and *flying* him into his seat. That would be in my better moments, but this isn't one of them. Stressed about the exit and about life in general, monster mom begins to appear as harshness peppers my words. By the time we are all in the car ready to go I realize I already lost the key that Sandra gave me less than five minutes ago. I'm right outside of her house!! How can I possibly lose the key?

But I can and I do. I have special skills in that department; it goes right along with my skill of getting lost. Frantically, angrily and with complete impatience I begin searching the car. I looked under the car. I back the car up to get a better view of under the car. I retrace my steps back to the side door from which we exited, desperately hoping that Sandra is already preparing for her workday and does not notice me. Dreading the conversation that would ensue if she did notice and came outside, "What are you doing?" "Well, ahhhh, I kind of dropped the key you *just* gave me and I cannot find it."

I have full confidence that her reply would be a gracious one, but I still don't want to find out. Fuming, I return to the car once more, make one more furious attempt to move this and pick up that and

On the River Boat tour in St. Louis, MO

look there, all to no avail. Muttering, mostly to myself but certainly in earshot of the kids, I express my utter discontent in an utterly unsanctified manner as we zoom off.

I know I am acting ridiculous. I know I am sinning. I know I would have to humble myself and ask my kids to forgive me. It's a battle between pride in the moment and future pride. The pride of not wanting to stop right now because it would require an immediate admittance of my sin versus the reality that I would have to admit my sin in the future anyway. Sadly, I opt to persist in the moment and it takes the 20+ minute drive to the Arch to finally calm down.

As I park the car I know I cannot continue with the day and act like all is well when there is a big ugly between my children and me. And I am the cause of the big ugly. It would be unfair and downright hypocritical to pretend that nothing happened and expect the kids to do the same. So swallowing the lump of pride in my throat, I turn to my eldest first, confessing that my anger was sinful, there was no excuse for it, it was wrong, and can she forgive me? Without hesitation, I hear, "yes." As I turn around to face my boys I ask the same question and get the same answer. Before I can even ask the final child I hear, "I forgive you too Mommy".

Oh, melt my heart Lord.

I am constantly amazed at how forgiving my children are, especially contrasted with how forgiving I am. There isn't a single influence on my life that has been as sanctifying as my children. I am confronted with my own shortcomings: anger that I want to soften as "frustration", impatience that I'd rather categorize as "just being tired" and selfishness disguised as "being overwhelmed". Being overwhelmed, getting tired and frustrated are all real in my life as a mom but I'd prefer to use them as excuses for sin instead of labeling sin properly and finding the freedom that only comes through repentance both to God and to the ones on the receiving end of my sin.

With a clean slate before the Lord and with my children, we embark on a day that turns into one of the most enjoyable days of our trip.

The kids earn another Junior Ranger badge, this time at the Jefferson Museum of Western Expansion, a fascinating place jam packed with

Cape Girardeau, MO at the Mississippi River

a wealth of information. Who knew that there was a museum UN-DER the Arch – as in **under**ground?

After badges, we pile into the tiny tram that slowly takes us to the top of the Arch. I feel like I'm in a submarine, except we are going up not down. I've never actually been on a sub though, so I guess I feel like I think I would feel in a submarine. After endless iterations of over two feet -- up two feet we reach the top and see some of the most amazing views. We can see the whole city. Yet within five minutes motion sickness from the swaying and claustrophobia from too many people kicks in; I grab each child by the collar as we gingerly find the exit.

It's a beautiful day so we head down to the river for a cruise along the mighty Mississippi. If you were to have a spy cam your footage would show four kids and one mom messily stuffing their faces with snacks as the boat cruises along. The novelty of the boat wears off rather quickly and the kids soon want to know when it will be over. Eventually it is. We make our way back up the boat ramp, pass under the Arch and cross through the construction filled intersection to arrive at the courthouse. Not just any courthouse. Apparently this courthouse has historic significance.

Slap "Historic Site" on a sign with an arrow and I'll be well on my way – I'm a total sucker for historic buildings, sometimes much to my kids' chagrin. I've come a long way since high school when I took all the A.P. history classes, but retained very little. Today provides an opportunity to fill in some of the many gaps in my historical understanding.

I certainly remember the name Dred Scott and know his court case was about slavery and his quest to win his freedom, but have no recollection that his case was first tried right here in St. Louis, MO.

Walking into the building I immediately feel small. I suspect it was designed that way on purpose. The dome ceiling in the center is intimidating and beautiful all at the same time. The building itself and the historical significance of this place are humbling. I am standing in the very building where Dred and Harriet Scott were treated as less than human.

We make our way into the very room where a judge sat and declared that these two people, despite being created in the image of God just like you and me, were merely property and without rights. Both anger and sadness pierce through my veins as I imagine that time in history. It sure makes my problems seem hardly worth mentioning when compared to their fight.

I try to imagine being them. Being told I am not human, or at best a lesser human. What a stark reminder of the depths of our sin.

It is tempting and easy to point a finger and say, "those people were so evil", but the reality is that I am just as evil. I am just as capable of error and of intentional wickedness. The only thing that differentiates me from "those people" whose sinful tendencies were more visible is the grace of God and the restraining power of the Holy Spirit in my life. Given the right conditions I am just as capable of equally deplorable sin.

As we travel from room to room, exploring the various displays and watching the different videos I do my best to instill in Abigail, my oldest, the weightiness of this trial and its implication on our country. With innocence that only comes with youth she simply cannot wrap her mind around why and how these people could be considered property. "Mom, that is so dumb" is her response to the idea that a man with darker skin could be considered less than human. If only everyone saw it so simply.

With that immensely humbling experience it's time to call it a day.

On the drive back to Sandra's house, my thoughts shift from Dred Scott and slavery to the key and what I am going to do and say. *I'm gonna have to come clean. I'll have to tell her I lost the key. And I have to be willing to absorb the cost if she decides to change her locks for safety sake. I am not looking forward to this!*

We pull up to the empty house. Sandra is delayed with client meetings and I am grateful for the extra time to procure a solution. I take a deep breath and do what I should have done the first time. "Lord, please help. Show me where the key is."

With one child sleeping I turn to the other three: "sit tight. I'm going to look for the key again." I open my door, get out of the car, squat down to examine the floor under my seat and what is that glistening in the reflection of the sun? A KEY! There it is. Under my seat. It must have fallen out of my pocket as I leaned in earlier to start the car before getting back out to buckle in my boys. There it was, all along. I could have listened to Abigail hours ago when she asked, "Is it on the floor mom?" I thought I had looked, but when one is in a rage rarely do the senses operate properly. And had I listened I would have missed out on the immensely humbling experience of acting like a baboon and having to repent. So all is well.

Introverted Twitching

March 20

In the morning we say our goodbyes and head out in search of Route 66. Since we are taking this massive trip we couldn't possibly pass up the opportunity to get our kicks on Route 66. Besides, how cool will I sound when I tell folks, "We took Route 66". Parachute pants cool for sure. My kids are slightly less enthusiastic. More specifically my copilot, aka Abigail, is less than thrilled. "Why are we looking for Route 66 *again*?" will be a common question over the next seven days.

Now, for one prone to getting lost nothing could possibly go wrong, right?

Finding 66 within St. Louis is more of a challenge than I anticipated so we eventually head to I-40 where I thought for sure there would be a sign. It would have been helpful at the outset to know that in this area Rt. 66 and I-40 are often one in the same with a few diversions off of the interstate, but such thorough preparation would be out of character. So the two hour trip by interstate takes over four as I seek to catch every Rt. 66 turn off. And for inquiring minds, no, it was not nearly as exciting as I thought it would be.

We eventually make it to our next destination; a family that, based on our email correspondance, seemed genuinely excited to have visitors. Not that the previous families were less than hospitable, but this family seemed different somehow. And my impression is quickly validated when we arrive.

I was given directions to their house not by street signs but by landmarks and mileage. "3.2 miles off of the exit you will see a gas station on the left and we are .2 mile after that on the right. The third driveway." We arrive to the address marked only by a mailbox and turn into a driveway not made of asphalt but by a path of worn grass extending back from the road.

We would soon grow accustomed to long driveways in out of the way locations. We seem to enjoy those visits the most.

Driving down the path, we pull past what looks to be the beginning of a fort made out of pallets on the left and a homemade tree swing on the right. The kids begin to bubble with eager anticipation.

There is an unofficial ritual that my boys follow as we approach each new home. A simple question is asked and the answer produces either elation or utter disappointment. "Mom, are there any boys?"

The first few times this question was asked I didn't know – I didn't remember. Quickly learning that, "I don't know" was not going to appease the passengers, I assigned Abigail the task of checking the email records to see what information we had on the family. Soon I would discover the immense benefits of having this information already available for when the question arose.

Today, both camps are elated with the response. Not only would my boys have a boy to play with, but also my girls would have a girl. It doesn't matter that the Jones' children are older by a few years – it's all about gender equity.

We pull up in front of the house and I take a guess at where we should park as the grassy driveway blends right in with the yard itself. I barely open my door before a cold wet schnoz is nuzzling its way in the crack to say hello. Whoops and hollers of excitement erupt from the back seat as not one but two dogs are spotted. Bounding out after the dogs are two young people offering polite hellos.

We make our way to the front door where Jennifer is there to open the door. The moment we walk inside I feel relaxed and comfortable. My eyes are immediately drawn to the walls that are covered with bookshelves which are filled with books. "Ah" I think to myself, "the mark of a homeschooler". The house itself is neat and organized. Not ornate by any means, but comfortable and warm. There are no young children in this home so I don't see any of the marks of life with a toddler, yet the orderliness is not intimidated. It's warming instead. Hospitable.

My love for books creates a magnetic effect and I can't wait for a moment to make my way over to the bookshelves to peruse. But first the pleasantries.

Jennifer and I sit and chat while the kids explore the outdoors. We talk about family and our Christian walk. About our goals for our children and our particular views on how to best achieve those goals. I am rather used to being "the strange one" when it comes to how I raise my children so it's a relief to sit and chat with someone who shares many of the same views. I find that I have an ally here who not only understands where I am coming from but is also coming from that same direction.

When Jennifer excuses herself to start on dinner I take the opportunity to check out the bookshelves. You can tell a lot about a person by the books they have in their home. What they read shows what they think about and what they value. Within the Christian genre, the types of theology books is often an indication of their theological leanings. I am always interested in the ratio of fluff to meat when it comes to the Christian books on the shelves and I always get excited when I can walk away and say "This could be my bookshelf". Such is the case today.

With sufficient insight into their reading habits, I figure I ought to help with dinner. Jennifer has a handle on everything and there isn't much for me to do so we continued our chat right where we left off. Soon enough Peter arrives home from work.

I never cease to be amazed at the depth and sweetness of fellowship I can have with the family of Christ, even upon our first meeting. To be embraced as family despite being strangers is unique to Christians because only Christians are part of a family that extends across the globe. My kids and I experience just that in home after home along our journey. When we converse, the topic is Jesus. He is the center of each discussion either overtly or as the underlying foundation.

As Christians, we live our lives to the glory of God. As parents, we seek to raise our children in the fear and admonition of the Lord. As workers, we work heartily as unto the Lord. With humility we admit our failings and share how Christ is working in our lives. We confess patterns of sin that the Holy Spirit has revealed to us and how, over time, we are being changed. We share our vision for our children and our grandchildren. It is such sweet fellowship.

With the meal now ready we transition from kitchen counter to dinner table and as the children file in from outside I'm pleasantly surprised by the absence of concern I have for my children's table manners, or lack thereof. For whatever reason, the lack of young children is not stirring in me a pride or fear of man which so often make me concerned about the opinions of others. I'm comfortable and content to simply partake of the meal and enjoy the conversation.

After dinner Peter prepares to lead his family in singing and Bible reading, as they do each evening. We are invited to join, but are not at all pressured. Once again we are delighted to participate and once again I am eager to see how another family does family worship.

Abigail frantically runs to the car to get her Bible and mine, afraid to miss even a moment. Pete Jr. blesses our ears musically on the piano as we sing "In Christ Alone" and other hymns. Then Peter opens the Word and reads for us. They seem to be going through Matthew verse by verse and tonight's text is about the woman caught in adultery. Peter uses discretion during his teaching for the benefit of little ears which do not yet fully understand what this sin means.

The Jones children are cheerfully involved in the discussion and it is clear that family Bible time is a delight to the whole family, not at all drudgery. What an encouragement to see first hand that instruction in the Word is a joy for these children. They are not sullen or bitter. They are not outwardly obedient but really stewing on the inside. It is an all around joy – and it means that the sweetness and eagerness I see in my children doesn't *have* to be a phase. It is not inevitable that they will eventually dread Bible reading. They may, but it doesn't have to be that way.

After Bible time, Peter takes all the kids outside for water balloon fun. My kids have a blast and I am quietly rejoicing on the inside as my children are seeing a father active in his kids' lives. Nothing about the night indicates that this was a show put on to impress us in any way. Every aspect seems to be the norm, from the warmness between Peter and Jennifer, the enjoyment brother and sister find in each other's company, the eagerness with which Bible time takes place to the games played afterwards. And all of it seems to go far beyond parental duty to enjoyment.

I'd like to say that I *always* enjoy my children, but the truth is I don't. And I suspect Peter and Jennifer have their moments too but the pattern of the home, the tone of the home indicates that they all genuinely enjoy each other's company. And that gives me hope.

A hope that the excitement I see in my children for God's Word doesn't have to be a phase. It doesn't have to go away when they reach the 'tween years, which is the age of the Jones' kids. The hope that the vision I have for my family is being lived out in other families and therefore it isn't as farfetched as some have tried to make me believe. Ultimately, this family points me back to our ultimate hope – Christ Jesus. He is the center of this family and it is evident.

In the morning, Peter and Jennifer work together to prepare a pancake feast. I don't know if this is their usual Saturday routine or if breakfast is more elaborate due to our visit. Either way, I soak up every moment of conversation with both of them. Our drive today is short in mileage, so there is no need to rush out the door, yet my introverted self begins to feel antsy. I don't want to overstay my welcome, but how do I know when is the "right time" to leave. I did let them know we'd be leaving sometime before noon and while I have enjoyed every minute of our stay, the extent of the interaction has been overwhelming.

After breakfast, I put my children on notice that they have an hour left to play. I say this as much for their benefit as for my own – it seems a more comfortable way to let Jennifer know our timetable for leaving. Why I don't turn directly to Jennifer and let her know what time we would be leaving, I'm not sure. This time, at least, I opt for a non-direct approach.

All of the children race outside for a few last turns with the bow and arrow while I pack up our things, including the sweet welcome note that was placed on my pillow yesterday. I place it in my bag alongside the note that Marsha included with the envelope of money from earlier on our trip.

Jennifer insists on packing us sandwiches and snacks for our drive and the entire Jones clan waves goodbye as we head back down the grass driveway -- all along wondering why I chose to leave so soon – why we didn't stay longer and enjoy more time with this wonderful family. What was it that caused my introverted twitching and the feeling that I need to breathe – away from other people. This trip is a series of trial and error episodes in which I begin to recognize that I do indeed have moments when I need a break from interacting with others, and slowly learn how to identify that need before it becomes overwhelming.

March 22

We jump back on Route 66 once *again*. I think we actually spend more time trying to *find* Route 66 than actually driving on it. The added *benefit* is that we just about doubled our travel time. So while I get the bragging rights of having driven Route 66, my kids get to endure a much longer car ride than is necessary or beneficial. But they live to tell the story, so no harm, right?

Our next network stay is all lined up until I receive an email saying the middle child came down with a stomach bug the night before. The Latham's are still willing to receive us but will understand if we don't want to stay. After our experience at the Harvey house I have no desire to be anywhere near a stomach bug and so I respond with a polite decline. But once again I'm left asking the Lord, "Now what?"

For now, we keep driving and after five solid hours we managed to squeak out just under 200 miles, thanks to good ole Route 66. It's the end to a rather pointless day and I find us a good deal on a hotel thanks to Priceline. As we make our way to the room the kids are giddy with excitement while my mind floods with all the cares and concerns of our situation.

All in all, the children still seem mostly oblivious to my almost constant mental anguish. Aside from knowing something is upsetting mom, they are clueless about the weight of it all -- the reality of our circumstances and the constant fear of being *found out* by one of the host families.

We are homeless. We are traveling from home to home, a night or two at a time, in an endless cycle. Each family we stay with knows that I am separated from my husband - I felt it important to let them know as the inevitable question of "Where is your husband?" would be thought, if not expressed verbally.

But I'm barely holding it together now. I could not handle people knowing any more than my preplanned spiel; "We are road schooling for a while". And it's true. We are. But that is an incomplete explanation. We are only road schooling because we have no home to homeschool in.

But the thought of the pity that would likely come from a family knowing the truth, or the disgust, or the expectation of additional information, a back-story, an explanation, some kind of logical plan for a very messy situation when I don't have *any* answers. I cannot go there even in my mind.

Instead, I'm filled with fear:

> What if my oldest slips and mentions we are homeless?
>
> What will the family think?
>
> What looks of disgust might we face?
>
> Will they think I am abusing the network?

While I ponder all of this, the kids bound from bed to bed with cheers and giggles. I would like to say I find their play entertaining. I wish I could say I respond well when they call out, "Mom, look at this" before trying a new trick. But the truth is far less flattering. I snap...at them. "Stop it!" "Be still!" "Be quiet, would you?"

I could excuse my response based on stress. Based on the fear that consumes me constantly. The fear of the unknown. Fear of the future. But to do so would be to justify my sin and there really is no justification for sin. It would be wrong. And it would be unfair to them. These four kids have been thrust into this crazy trip and despite constant adjustments are doing marvelously. They certainly don't deserve my anger. Yet at the same time I cannot shake it.

I need to remind myself, often, that this trip is exactly the kind of thing I would do. Had I planned six months ago and told my closest friends, "We are taking an open ended road trip in March" their response would not at all be surprise but rather, "Awesome! That's so like you." Same trip just different circumstances.

An intentional departure with meticulous planning would have been my preference, but instead our departure was by default and the planning is on the fly. So what? Why let the circumstances ruin an otherwise awesome experience. A simple change in mindset can greatly reduce the anguish. We GET to take an epic road trip - the envy of almost every homeschooler. We have no timetable. No job to return to dictating an end date. There are no external factors influencing where or when or what, not even financially.

The reality is I have the same income as before. I am doing the same job I did before - just remotely. The job causes other stress, but my income is the same and yet my expenses are drastically decreased. With no rent, no utilities and food mostly taken care of by host families I have more discretionary income than ever before which allows us to do and see things that would never have been in the budget in the past. And most importantly, I have the same God - the same Heavenly Father who is my ultimate Provider and who is guiding every step of this journey.

So after a firm scolding from myself I jump into the fun and wrestle the kids before we turn in for the night.

March 23

It's Sunday. Church day. With very rare exceptions, the kids have always associated Sunday with church because that's where we would be. But today I have no desire to go. No desire to "be on" - to answer all of the standard first-time-visitor questions. I go through the same set of questions with each new family, which surprisingly I haven't minded much, but it still drains me. The amount of interaction I have had with people has been draining. Oh, don't get me wrong, everyone has been kind and hospitable and perfectly pleasant. But I can only handle so much at a time and this trip is keeping me right at my limit.

The original Tow Mater. Galena, KS

Lost Baggage and Perfect Strangers

March 27

Little Rock is a bit of a disappointment. I'm not sure why I keep putting cities on our agenda expecting something spectacular. I'm not much of a city girl -- if you can even consider some of these places actual cities. I grew up a train ride away from "the city," New York and went to college in the city of brotherly love, Philadelphia. Many of the so-called cities we have visited are not much larger than my hometown. Nonetheless my brain says, "Well, you are traveling through Arkansas; of course you need to visit the capital city."

Now for my kids, any place with a decent park is worth a stop. Long driving days are made bearable by the promise of a park before the day is done. But we can't even find that here. Not a single playground comes up on our map searches nor is sighted during our park-hunting drives. Equally frustrated by the lack of results, Abigail asks why they don't like kids here. "What do you mean?" I ask in reply. "Well, there aren't any playgrounds. If they liked kids they would have some playgrounds." Makes perfect sense from a kids perspective, but from my perspective they don't like parents. If they did then surely there would be an abundance of playgrounds to which moms and dads can take their kids so energy can be expended. Or maybe I'm just tired and cranky.

After more than a reasonable amount of time hunting for a park, I give up and head back to our hotel. It's barely noon and I need something to keep the kids engaged for the next seven hours before I can announce bedtime. I have little endurance today for the childishness of my children as once again, all my mental and emotional capacities seem full with the cares and concerns of day-to-day life. But kids will be kids and to expect them to be otherwise is unrealistic. My kids, in this moment, need to get the wiggles out. So we take a walk.

We start inside the hotel but within five minutes we've covered every floor and hallway – even the vending areas. So we head outdoors for some fresh air and maybe some lunch. We just start walking up and down the streets adjacent to the hotel. Are there no restaurants around here? We don't go much more than three or four blocks in any direction because I'm prone to getting lost and because I don't want to take any chances that we meander into an area that isn't safe. I'm tired of sitting in the car but I'm also hungry, as are the four little people with me. Where are we going to eat? There isn't even a grocery store to grab some bread for sandwiches.

As we head back down a side street towards the hotel, we see a trolley-stop sign. Perfect! There is a trolley due in just a few minutes. It will take us all the way through the city. We can hop off to eat somewhere. And best of all, I get to sit down while the kids get the excitement of riding on something. And if nothing else will bring us a few hours closer to bedtime.

*****

With five full tummies, the trolley heads back over the bridge to return us to our starting point. The trolley driver/tour guide casually mentions that a college baseball game will be taking place tonight, "right over there". Right over there happens to be right next to our hotel. "Tickets are only three-bucks and the kids would love it," he tells us. But maybe it isn't such a casual comment. Does he get a cut of ticket sales?

I am quite indifferent to watching any baseball game, especially a game for a college team that I do not follow. But if the children will be happy three-bucks a head is a small price to pay. Besides, there is a bounce house section towards the back of the ballpark that the kids eyed earlier today. That's the real reason for attending the game – the kids will have a blast. So after dinner we head over to buy our tickets. By this time they are so very excited at the prospect of bouncing. By this time, I am so very tired and still overwhelmed. I still feel like I'm recovering from over-socialization (yup, totally made up that word) and from the constant demands of caring for four children while on the road. All I want is some peace and quiet and bouncy houses will give me just that – my kids will have their much needed energy outlet and I'll have some downtime.

I should have known better.

Firstly, I walk up to the ticket counter to be knocked over with sticker shock. $42 for all of us – so much for $3 a ticket. I begrudgingly hand over my debit card, knowing that in my kids' minds this was already a done deal. In this rather wimpy parenting moment, I'd rather fork over **$42** than deal with the unhappy responses of my children if we left and went back to the hotel.

Oblivious and/or indifferent to the cost, all four kids are as happy as can be as they skip into the park. I walk a step behind mumbling to myself and already regretting this decision. But the worst is yet to come.

As soon as we pass through the gates and into the park the kids make a b-line to the Kids Zone where the bounce houses are set up -- only to discover that Kids Zone is NOT included in the price of admission. You have got to be kidding me. The only reason we are attending this stupid game is to play in the kids area. I don't give two licks about the teams playing. It's cold and windy. I'm freezing. I don't even know who is playing. We are in this city because it's supposed to be fun yet I'm not having any fun here. I just wasted $42 and now I'm supposed to pay an EXTRA $3 **per kid** so they can play??

I am totally put out and not at all friendly. My kids just know that mom told them they would get to play tonight. In their minds, we're here, so what's the hold up? My sweet Abigail gently tugs on my shirt, "Mom, I have $6. I can pay for some of us." "I have $3 Mom. I'll buy my own ticket," Annabella says after her. "FINE!" I shout. "Go ahead. I'm not paying another single penny in this park. Go ahead if you want to."

The girls come back with three tickets, leaving us one short. I'm still too angry and too caught up in my own selfishness to care much. The assumption, of course, is that Abigail bought Austin's ticket since he is the youngest. "What about me, Mom?" asks a tearful Alexander. "What about you? Do you have three dollars?" I snap. Between shoulder heaving sobs he says, 'No. I don't have any money.'

I wave the other three off. "Go, go play. You bought your tickets. Go!" With Alexander still crying beside me the other three take off excitedly. Then Abigail stops and turns around. She is clearly unsure. She wants to play. She has a ticket. But what about her brother? She slowly returns to where I am standing with her tearful brother and asks, "should I give my ticket to Alexander?"

The depth of my pride seems bottomless. When I think it can go no deeper another situation arises in which I prove myself wrong – I can be even more prideful. I've been screaming at my four kids for the last 15 minutes not because they have done anything wrong. Not because they are being disobedient or otherwise sinful. And not that any of that would even justify my screaming. But nope, I'm yelling at my kids because I made a poor decision. I'm yelling at my kids because I made a commitment to them BEFORE I knew what that commitment would cost and instead of admitting that error I persisted in foolishness and am now taking it out on them.

But in an instant, when faced with the sweet kindness of my eldest child, willing to sacrifice her enjoyment for her brother, I broke. "Ah, I'm so sorry. I'm acting so very unkind. No, Abigail, you shouldn't give him your ticket, but I am so proud of you for offering. I should buy his ticket. We came so you could play. Let's go play." And with joyfulness unmatched brother and sister skip toward the ticket table so that the last of the children can join the fun.

*****

Morning comes way too soon. A new day of travel. A new day of the same old stresses. I wish the days were shorter and the nights longer. Still, this new day requires action like all the others. We must move on and I am eager to get to our next destination – but only after we make a quick stop.

Little Rock has certainly been a disappointment and a money pit due to my foolishness, but we can't come to Little Rock and not visit the infamous high school. The very site where nine brave black young people courageously entered Little Rock High School to break segregation in the schools. I have read about this place in textbooks. I've seen the black and white photo of the scene during various history classes over the years. But living thousands of miles away geographically and a million miles away culturally the significance of this event has always been lacking. I knew intellectually it was a big deal but quite honestly, I didn't really care. I may have feigned

Outside of Pythian Castle, Springfield, MO

care because I was probably supposed to care, but in my teenage mind this had absolutely nothing to do with me.

We pack up the car once again, jamming our over-night bags into every nook and cranny of the cargo bag hanging off the back of the car. I had hoped that the rear hanging option would give us better gas mileage than a roof top carrier. It probably has, but at the sacrifice of not having access to the car hatch. It has pretty decent storage capacity, but the constant opening and closing of the bag, removing of items and fitting them back in is cumbersome. And so our packing system is ever evolving. Maybe by the end of the trip I'll have the perfect system.

We head out from the hotel following the directions on my phone. How did people travel pre-smart phones? I suppose there was much more planning involved; mapping out the route with a highlighter. I suspect there was less, "we'll figure it out on the way" and more, "let's make sure we know exactly where we are going." Travel could commence without any concern for loss of navigation due to cell dead zones. And one actually gained a skill in trip preparations, the skill of reading a map, versus the skill of listening to Siri say, "Turn left in .6 miles."

Anyway, as I follow the phone directions we come around a bend that immediately turns into a steep climb followed by an abrupt decent with more speed than is safe. As we pop over this unexpected hill I hear a deafening THUD as the car jolts. Thinking about both the roof top carrier and the rear carrier I begin to ponder with dread what damage has been done to my car from this one hill. It's like a speed bump on steroids, yet traveling way beyond speed bump speed.

In the silence following the thud, I listen closely for any indication of the damage - as if I know anything about cars other than where the ignition is and how often to change the oil. But I do know the sound of a flat tire, and thankfully that sound is absent. So I ignorantly ignore my concern and continue on to the destination, only a few more miles down the road.

We arrive at a vacant school; not a single car is on the street or in the parking lot. We seem to be catching spring break everywhere we go.

In other places it's less than desirable because no school means that parents are taking their kids to many of the spots we are trying to visit. Today, however, it doesn't bother me one bit. There will be no witnesses as this dorky tourist gets out of her clearly not urban vehicle with Yankee plates to take a picture of a school.

One of my goals in homeschooling is to bring history to life for my children. To expand upon the textbook learning of dates and facts and help them think deeply and really process the past – basically the opposite of my experience in history classes. And unlike my apathetic view towards the civil rights time in our history, my hope is that my children will not only learn the who, what, where and when of history, but also the why so they can also learn the why not. What is wrong and what is right and what do they need to do today, in their lifetime, to strive for right and stand up against wrong.

That is a tall order considering my kids are 8 and under. The older two have a vague understanding of segregation but don't at all understand the why. To them it is dumb. Basically the same assessment as in St. Louis with Dred Scott. Why separate people because of their skin color? It is dumb, plain and simple. A child can see that. And it is dumb, to put it mildly. And other than the depravity of man, I don't have much of an explanation for them. But one day, maybe, as we study this time period in our nation's history I can look at them and say, "you were there."

Learning history from a book can be so very dry and boring. But to see the sites, to be on location and allow your imagination to run with questions like, "What was it like at that time?" "Who might have been walking this way?" "What would I have done?" Questions like that bring history alive for me, and my hope is it will do the same for my children as we see and experience aspects of our country on this trip. To go beyond learning the "material" and realize what is a subject matter for us was life for the people living it. And now their lives are our history.

We pull up in front of the vacant school and I sigh as I imagine what that day was like. I should say I try to imagine -- I could never, never understand what that day was like. Certainly not for those children nor for the majority skin color: those that were outright racist, those caught in a mob mentality following the crowd and those with a hatred for racism but with no power to do anything about it. Sadly, I suspect that last group was a small group.

This is literally a drive by stop. Mom has an agenda and that agenda includes getting down to Hot Springs by noon. For the sake of nostalgia, I decide to take a picture. It doesn't seem appropriate to have the kids pose with smiling faces at a location with such a sordid history, so I step out of the car solo and snap a picture of the school. "One day", I think to myself and probably say out loud, "I will show this to the kids and say, 'you were here'".

As I turn and begin to walk back around the front of the car to my door I notice the rear storage bag looks funny. Walking nearer, the scene slowly comes into full view: the bag is sidewise, hanging from a single strap. "Oh my! That THUD we heard was the weight of this massive bag banging against my back bumper after the buckle snapped. Oh, and a piece of my car flying off as well - I suspect from the weight and force of it all."

"Great," I growl and then "great" I say with all sincerity.

"Thank you Lord! Had we not stopped here I would not have seen this. And had I not seen this we would be driving down the interstate at 60+ mph with the bag half hanging off. And who knows then if the other strap would break heaving half of our belongings down the road." With my best MacGyver impression I tie the flailing strap, hoping to secure it long enough to find a replacement. All the while I can't help but marvel at God's goodness, His timing, and His grace. As annoying as this is, it could have been much, much worse.

*****

A few hours later, we arrive in Hot Springs. The town itself is rather cheesy and has a very touristy feel. But that doesn't bother me much because I am more interested in the nearby mountain. It has been way too long since we've taken a good hike, but the drizzle in the air and the dark clouds in the sky put a damper on my plans. As much as I enjoy hiking, I have no desire to do so at the risk of being stuck deep in the woods, in a rainstorm, with four young kids -- at least two of whom would almost assuredly find no joy in hiking in the rain and desire that I carry them back to the car. So this too will be a quick stop.

Despite the name of the town, Hot Springs, I am somehow ignorant of the fact that there are actual, real, literal h-o-t s-p-r-i-n-g-s here. Along the sidewalk between our car and the visitors center are fountains of near-boiling water. Plunging my hand into this uncomfortably warm water is what finally connects the information - Hot Springs *HAS* Hot Springs.

After gathering an area map and some other bits of information and trying to dodge the increasing raindrops we hop back into the car. If we can't hike at least we can drive through the mountain for a while.

It's an interesting mountain. There is no main entrance and no main parking lot. Rather there are smaller pull-offs at random intervals where you can park and hike. We have only passed a handful of cars and the current pull-off is completely vacant. The rain is holding off to a midst and I'm growing antsy. "Who wants to hike?" I ask, hoping to get better than a 50% response. Instead I get one enthusiastic yes, one hesitant yes, as if I twisted her arm, one grumpy grunt indicating no and one non-answer. That's good enough for me.

Truth be told, as long as I had one of them on my side, we were going hiking.

Once I get everyone out of the car and we start moving towards the trail, the mood of the group improves with three of the four now enthusiastic. (I knew I could turn them!) The grumpy child remains grumpy but that is not going to deter me. We head out over logs and through the woods; climbing anything is a mood enhancer for my crew. It's a rather pleasant temperature for a hike so I don't mind the mist.

As far as I can tell there is no loop to take, so I have to gauge how far we have gone and make sure the little legs accompanying me will have enough juice to propel themselves back to the car from wherever we decide to turn around. I can handle carrying the smallest child if need be, and maybe another in a piggy back, but that is the limit!

We do eventually retreat and just as we arrive back at the car I notice a younger fellow - maybe early 20's, across the road with a handsome dog on a leash. Apparently it's a pleasant temperature for a dog walk as well.

He crosses over just as I open the rear door to load up my boys. "Do you have any water?" He asks. "For you, or for the dog?" I inquire, wondering if a fresh water bottle is required or if I can offer the half-empty bottle in the door. "For the dog."

I grab the half-empty (or half-full for all you optimists) bottle and an empty cup. The dog won't mind the crumbs from yesterdays snack, I'm sure. Pouring the water into the cup I squat down to hold it for the dog. He wastes no time in drinking. "We've been out all afternoon, I didn't realize how far we were from camp and I didn't bring him any water," the young man offers. "No worries. He is cute."

"It looks like you are traveling. Are you staying at one of the camp grounds here?"

That's the second time he's mentioned campgrounds - I didn't realize there were any here. But with that second mention my radar goes off and my self-defense training kicks into high gear.

I'm still squatting with the dog: a flood of thoughts go through my mind as I begin to gaze left and right without appearing nervous.

Okay, We are very isolated.

There are no other cars around

Haven't seen a single other soul. No one would hear me if I screamed

He is athletic.

He has a dog with him - a conversation starter. Common ploy by psycho murderers

He has ascertained that we are traveling therefore there is no one waiting on us, no one else in our party

I'm a single woman with four children. Lots of vulnerability.

All of these thoughts shoot through my brain in rapid succession and almost as quickly it becomes clear that this conversation needs to end and we need to leave, as soon as possible but as naturally as possible. Either he is a psycho murderer and we have little time to get out of here or he is a normal guy just making conversation and would be highly offended if he had any idea the thoughts in my brain.

"He is quite cute", I say, rising back upright as I give the dog a firm pat. Despite the cute doggy just begging to be pet, the children are already in the car, the significance of which would continue to sink in as I debrief myself later. I return the water bottle and cup back into the car through the door that is still ajar and then shut it, hoping that would bring an end to the encounter and we would part ways.

"Thanks again for the water" he says as he gently pulls on the leash to direct the dog to follow back the way they came. I climb into the driver's seat, lock the doors and start the car. After a deep breath of relief I pull out of the parking spot and head down the mountain. We are all done with hiking for today.

Old Friends Like Warm Socks
– or Something Like That

March 28

Up to this point I haven't shared much with any of the families about my situation and anything I did share was rather vague. Certainly no one knows the reality of our trip, at least not from my own lips. I do often wonder what folks really think and how much they can ascertain, I mean who really needs as much stuff as we have for a mere roadtrip, but I'd like to believe I'm rather stealth in my delivery of "the story" – after all, I long had aspirations of being a U.S. Marine.

Fantasy aside, folks have been told this is a "road trip" and we are "headed out to California to visit my brother and sister-in-law". Having a destination (California) seems to give our trip a bit of structure, at least in my head, and improves my cover story. We are visiting family - no one would question that. And we are home-schoolers - every homeschooler either has taken a road trip or dreams of taking one. So this random, open ended, meandering trip seems a little less odd when the destination is defined and we are simply "seeing as much as we can between here and there".

As we pull into the driveway of an old friend from my Mississippi days my plan remains the same. "We are homeschoolers - what homeschooler hasn't wanted to take an epic road trip? We are blessed to be able to do this and are headed out to visit my brother and sister-in-law. We want to see as much as we can along the way."

Now Angela and her husband Jack already know more than most. They knew when my husband left -- one of the handful of friends from Mississippi that I've kept in touch with and from whom I've asked for prayer. But they don't know that we are currently home-less. They don't know that everything we own is inside of and on top of our car. They don't know that I have no plan and have no idea what I'll be doing a week from now. I didn't come to put any of that on them; we are here simply to spend time with an old friend. And besides, immense embarrassment makes sticking *to the story* much more appealing than full disclosure.

Now Angela is a master organizer and as I mention in conversation that I am constantly repacking the car to make more room she offers her services. So we head out to the car and I begin to unload the back. What can fit on top, what needs to be readily accessible and what can be tucked away in the recesses of the car? We discuss all of this as she helps me develop a game plan. "Half of our stuff is homeschool material," I say with a slight laugh, hoping it doesn't seem too bizarre to be traveling all this way with so many books. I offer further explanation hoping it will remove all curiosity, "I planned to keep up with our study schedule along the way but quickly realized that was insane. I don't think we've even cracked a book." "Have you thought about sending some things home to make more room?" she replies, quite logically. "Just the things you won't need for a while?"

I'm stuck. My brain cannot come up with a reasonable reply and I have no desire to mislead a friend anyway. Her perfectly logical reply deserves an equally logical response. "Truth is, Angela, this is everything we own. We are not returning to NY."

Everything in me wants to leave it at that and hope that social dictates about proper conversation would prevent her from asking for clarification. But I can't do that to a friend. I know I need to say more and am glad to finally be forced to say it. "Things blew up where we were staying and it was no longer a healthy environment for the kids and me. We are traveling to figure out where we want to go. I'm ready to find a place where we have a solid church that is willing and able to come along side of us and mentor my boys. We didn't have that in NY and now more than ever I am so aware of how important that is."

There, I said it. It's out there now. Best of all, I survived. Nothing fell out of the sky to squash me. A giant wooden mallet did not come across the scene like a pendulum to send me flying in the opposite direction. Nor did any other Looney Tunes inspired scenes play out to end my existence. To say the words was not nearly as painful as I expected and the lack of shock and horror on Angela's end surely helped in that regard.

*****

When I think hospitality I immediately think food. If I am going to extend hospitality part of that planning, much of that planning is centered around a meal. What should I offer? And what if they don't like it? What if they leave thinking that meal was the most disgusting thing they've ever eaten?

With a handful of exceptions, I don't remember the meals we have eaten from house to house. I remember the Mac n' Cheese made special order for my son's 5th birthday. There were noodle dishes of various kinds at many of the homes because that was the kid safe response I gave when asked what we would like to eat – "noodles". I remember scrambled eggs for a few breakfasts and PB&J lunches made for us at two houses to take with us for the day. And I remember pizza this night – because of the simplicity of it. Because it reminded me that fellowship is about the people, not about the food. So while I know that we *did* eat at each and every house, I have little recollection of *what* we ate.

This night it is pizza. Domino's delivery to be specific. The food is as you would imagine from Domino's take out -- the blessing of this visit clearly isn't the food. Nope, it's the time with Angela and her children, the encouragement I receive (and hopefully also give) the fun my kids have with new friends, mostly playing superhero dress up. The food was just something to fill our stomachs, but the time of fellowship is what filled our souls.

How Not to Do It

March 29

We are on our own tonight. I tried to line up a network stay but to no avail. No one south and no one west are available to host us, so we will head down from Arkansas to Louisiana. Not sure what we'll do in Louisiana. We are nowhere near New Orleans, and I'm not too sure I'd want to visit there even if it were close. There appears to be a free ferry that can take us from Louisiana into Galveston, Texas, which is where we plan to head tomorrow anyway. The kids would get a kick out of a ferry ride for sure. I can't find the ferry schedule online so for now we'll just start heading south and see what we see along the way – hopefully we can figure out the ferry when we get to Port Arthur, which is the departure city.

Thus far Priceline has been my go-to for hotels. We haven't had a single problem and we've been able to stay in a few very nice hotels that I would not have been able to afford otherwise, including one where breakfast was far superior to the usual semi-edible fare. As I figure out how much driving we can reasonably do today my co-pilot is on the Priceline app reading me hotel reviews. We find what sounds like a decent one, about an hour from where we currently are. Perfect! We will arrive with plenty of time to have a leisurely dinner before settling to bed.

When we do arrive we see a packed parking lot. It appears that a wedding is going on and I wonder how many drunken neighbors we will have tonight. But that is the least of my concerns after I step up to the reception desk and hear, "Ma'am, we have no rooms. Priceline has been overbooking us all day and we are simply full."

Wonderful. What does this mean for their no-refund policy? Am I stuck with the bill *and* with no hotel room because they messed up?

I get on the phone with Joey, a customer service representative who denies responsibility on behalf of Priceline. I am less than happy. Thankfully, after the desk clerk confirms the story, he issues my refund. But now what? I still have nowhere to stay tonight, it's getting late and I'm tired of driving. After being assured of the refund we head out and begin to drive, yet again. "We might as well head west toward Texas," I say to my co-pilot sitting in the seat next to me, "let's start searching for hotels."

It's not a lack of options; there are plenty of hotels. The trick is finding one in my price range that is half decent. If I wasn't traveling with kids I'd be less selective -- I can bear almost any condition for a night or two, if needed. But with four young children I do not want to worry about the condition of the room. Part of our hotel-finding process includes my co-pilot plugging in our minimum requirements. We want at least 2-stars and at least a 3-out-of-5 rating from customers. From there we start reading off customer reviews.

Like any review process, there are always disgruntled people. So when a hotel has a good ranking and good reviews with an occasion lambaste from a former customer I take it with a big grain of salt. Usually it's someone who seemed to have expected 5-star conditions at a 2-star hotel. But most customer reviews are very helpful.

I don't care about the decor of the hotel but was the room clean? I generally ignore comments about breakfast because I don't expect anything gourmet from a 2-star hotel. I don't even expect anything edible. I assume it's the standard budget hotel food that will leave us feeling ill, and anything better than that is a nice surprise. But it can be hard to sleep when there is a stink of some sort, so does anyone mention an odor?

It's that last question I should have paid more attention to as we searched out another hotel.

My co-pilot finds a hotel that seems to meet all of our criteria and is in our price range. It's about 90 minutes away, which is the maximum I want to drive at this point. There is one comment that raises some concern, but I push it aside as a disgruntled customer.

"I booked a non-smoking room only to arrive and be told that they only have smoking rooms - not happy!"

I have my daughter re-read the hotel description: "38-non smoking rooms".

He must be mistaken, I say to myself. *Maybe he has a beef to pick with someone there. It is clearly a non-smoking hotel.*

"Book it," I say with a gusto that is simply fun -- our teamwork at this point is flawless and her little finger navigates through the app to book a room.

We arrive and check in without incident. We head upstairs to our room and I see the symbol on the door to our room - clearly marking this a smoking room. "Maybe we won't notice," I think optimistically as I hesitantly open the door. As soon as we step in the odor is evident. "Mom, it smells in here," my oldest states matter of factly. "It smells like smoke."

I give my kids the standard "don't touch anything" command while I grab a baby wipe out of our toiletry bag to clean off the phone before picking up the receiver. I dial the main desk. "Hi, you just checked us in. We are supposed to be in a non-smoking room, but this one is clearly smoking."

"I'm sorry, I'll see what I can do," she replies in a less than convincing tone.

"Should we change Mom?"

"No, we are not staying in this room. Don't move, don't touch anything."

It's been five minutes and I haven't heard back. With the distinct feeling of being put-off I decide we aren't waiting any longer. "Let's go guys, grab the bags."

We head downstairs to the desk where the lady, Carmen, is standing. She's not on the phone talking to anyone in an attempt to rectify my situation, neither is she on her computer looking at the bookings for the night to find a vacant room. "She clearly was ignoring us. She had no intention of fixing this!" I say to myself while trying to put on a pleasant face.

It's 9:00pm. I'm tired, I'm stressed. I just want to be done for the night. I realize this likely isn't her fault, she just works here. Nevertheless, this is the second Priceline mess-up today and I need someone to take responsibility.

As I approach the desk it's like she was waiting for me, knowing I'd be coming at some point.

"I am sorry, ma'am, we don't have any more non-smoking rooms."

"I booked a non-smoking room. I have 4 kids, we cannot stay in a smoking room. So if you don't have another room I'd like a refund." I have no desire to beat around the bush at this point.

She calls her boss, the owner. I can tell as I listen in that this is not going to end in my favor. "My boss says that you aren't guaranteed a non-smoking room."

"Well, actually I am. I booked a non-smoking room."

This gets nowhere so I call Priceline directly. By now it is 9:30pm and I just want to go to sleep.

"Hi. I have a problem and I am hoping you can help me. Earlier today I was overbooked by you guys into a hotel, so I rebooked at a different hotel. I just checked into that hotel. It was supposed to be a non-smoking room but it's smoking and the desk clerk says they have no more non-smoking rooms."

I was strategic in the words I chose and mindful of my tone. With my business background I know some of the trigger words and phrases that increase the chance of a favorable outcome. Any half-decent customer service department would immediately assume proper responsibility and rectify the situation one way or another. Let that be a spoiler for how this turns out.

"I'm sorry ma'am. We don't overbook. That hotel must not have updated the information once they were full." ::pause:: *not true. I had a fairly lengthy conversation with that first hotel clerk and have had another such conversation with a clerk at another hotel who provided behind the scenes information on how it all works. The hotel does not do the updating -- Priceline has direct access to that information, they simply ignored it and booked anyway.* back to the lies... "as for this hotel, when you book your room you are not guaranteed smoking preference."

"I understand that, but this is listed as a non-smoking hotel. So there shouldn't be any smoking rooms. In a non-smoking hotel there is no concern about getting placed in a smoking room because it is not possible."

"The website does not explicitly state non-smoking."

"Sir, Carmen here, the desk clerk, has confirmed that they have 37 rooms at this location. The website indicates 38 non-smoking rooms. By definition that is a non-smoking hotel."

We go back and forth for a while. I tell him I am traveling with 4 young children, it is now 10pm and we have no hotel room because of Priceline's errors. I remind him this is the second incident today, for which he once again places blame on the hotel. I let him know that I have used Priceline numerous times over the last few weeks and will be staying in quite a few more hotels in the upcoming weeks. I have been pleased up until today, but this is inexcusable. To which he replies with a lame, "I am sorry." Thankfully I resist the urge to scream, "NO, YOU ARE NOT SORRY. IF YOU WERE SORRY YOU WOULD REFUND MY MONEY AND BOOK ME INTO ANOTHER HOTEL FOR FREE, JUST TO MAKE IT UP TO ME!"

Instead, I say that if they cannot rectify the situation they are going to lose a customer -- another strategic sentence that most companies train their employees to respond to. Instead he is content to let me go.

What a contrast -- we are receiving tremendous hospitality from home to home as we travel. These families are receiving no financial benefit from our stay and actually incur expenses with extra water, food, etc. Yet here are two businesses in the hospitality *industry* that have failed miserably at any attempt to be hospitable.

This is the very last time we use Priceline.

I thank the desk clerk again, who was kind enough to bring out snacks for my tired and hungry crew at some point during my phone call. I tell her that I know it's not her fault.

It's so easy to yell at customer service people, and yelled at they are. But they don't set the policies and they don't make the rules. They have the unfortunate task of upholding the policies and rules, no matter how illogical or unhelpful those rules may be.

Carmen tries to convince me to stay as the room is already paid for, but I decline again stating that I have four young children, whom she can clearly see, and I cannot stay in a room that reeks of smoke.

If a wave of nausea didn't come over me when we entered the room I might have considered it, but principle is also on the line. The basic principle of honesty. One company refuses to take responsibility for the information that is on their own website and another clearly doesn't have an ethical issue with lying. Remember that review I ignored? I'm not the first person to have an issue here. The woman who owns this facility has false information on the website, she promotes her hotel as a non-smoking facility yet has smoking rooms. I doubt my silent protest will make any difference in her moral compass, especially since she already has my money, but at least I made my stand.

So we get back in the car, once again hunting for a hotel -- this time as a hotels.com convert.

I Scream, You Scream. Blue Bell factory tour, Brenham, TX

The Little Things are Sometimes the Big Things

April 4 –

The last few days have been enjoyable. We've visited Kemah Boardwalk in Houston, TX where the kids got to enjoy a few rides. They pretended to be future astronauts at the Houston Space Center and I lost our stroller when it fell off the trolley that transported us around during the official tour (I guess I should have listened to the man when he told me "No strollers on the tour.") We also toured the Blue Bell Ice Cream factory and enjoyed every bit of our oversized sample afterward. But my personal highlight from the past few days is hands down receiving a sewing lesson that resulted in quite a cute dress, if I do say so myself. The last house we stayed at was chock full of rather skillful seamstresses and the lady of the house gave me my first full sewing lesson.

She first made a skirt for my oldest daughter as I looked on and then walked me through making a whole dress for my second daughter as I did the labor. I was nothing short of astonished when it was complete and everything lined up properly. I've never done much sewing in my life other than replacing a button or mending the back of various stuffed animals that needed surgery, so this was such a treat. The kids have experienced a number of "firsts" - this was my first big "first", and what a kindness from God. Now I can't wait to get my own sewing machine.

God continues to demonstrate kindness to me in so many unexpected ways. I shouldn't be surprised, because that is indeed His character, however I am so very aware of my unworthiness, and still have lots of lingering self-righteousness that says I must *earn* God's kindness. I do not at all *deserve* anything kind or good from the Lord, but He continues to lavish me with His kindness and at the next house it would overflow in the most wonderful ways to my son.

As we near our destination, I'm awed by the size and extravagance of the homes we are passing. We have experienced such a range of homes on our journey and it's exciting each and every time to see what awaits. "Horses on the right," I call out. Scouting for animals as we drive never seems to get old - cows and horses are the most common, a few goat sightings as well. A horse is a horse is a horse - at least to a bunch of New Yorkers. And from the distance of where our car drives and where the animals are I can't much tell the difference between them. Yet all of us, myself included, eagerly turn our heads to get a glimpse at each animal we pass.

We enter into their subdivision now and Abigail asks a most logical question based on what we have seen on the last few streets, "Do you think this family will have horses, Mom?"

Just a few minutes later we pull into their driveway. It is a magnificent house with, from what I can tell, quite a bit of land - but this coming again from a New Yorker for whom a half-acre is living

Austin in, well, Austin... TX.
We couldn't pass up the opportunity to take our Austin to Austin, TX.
And here is the picture to prove it.

large. No horses, but that disappointment quickly fades when we are greeted by a friendly dog who seems to have heard us arrive. Tail wagging and tongue slobbering, he comes bounding around the side of the house with a bounce in his step. We are halfway to the front door when Debbie Petroski makes her way outside, "Oh, your husband isn't with you?" She seems as shocked at his absence as I am at the question. "Nope," I reply with a smile, "just us." "I guess she didn't read my profile," I muse silently as Debbie welcomes us inside.

My kids are quick to find her youngest two children as well as the toys in the backyard. I am constantly awed by how quickly my kids adapt from house to house and more than once the hostess has stated that their level of comfort is wonderful. I'm glad that seems to be the consensus amongst our hosts because I often wonder if it comes across as rude.

Debbie asks if I need a hand bringing in our bags. My instinct is to say no. My instinct is to always say no when asked if I need help. But she persists in such a sweet way that to not allow her to help seems inappropriate, so we walk back out the front door together making small talk. "You asked about my husband," I say, wanting to clarify right away, "I put it in my profile, but he left 2 1/2 years ago." "I didn't even read your profile but oh, I'm sorry," offers Debbie with all sincerity, "sadly that is all too common these days."

What could have been an awkward start to an awkward stay turned into a wonderful time of transparency, on both sides.

Debbie and I retrieve the bags from the car for our two night stay and she takes me to our room. It's their eldest daughter's room, who is away for a few weeks; a bunk bed with additional floor space and a bathroom right outside the bedroom door, which will be just for us.

We have stayed in homes that shared a single bathroom for their family of 9 in addition to our family of 5. It works and I have no complaints. How can I really complain when I'm being offered hospitality? But I'm sure it's no surprise that it is wonderful when a family is able to offer us a bathroom, reserved just for us. Such a luxury provides an additional level of comfort and a nice privacy barrier that this introvert especially appreciates.

Now tomorrow is Alexander's birthday. He is so excited to turn 5 and I am so excited to celebrate another year of God's goodness to him and to our family. But I don't for a second want to impose upon our hosts and make them feel in any way that they need to acknowledge his birthday. So on the drive here the kids were thoroughly warned about slipping – "now listen guys, I know tomorrow is Alexander's birthday. We are *not* going to mention that to this family. We will figure out a way to celebrate his birthday, but it is not this family's responsibility to celebrate the birthday. Got it?" "Okay Mom" came the response in chorus, in obedience, but not with much eagerness.

Well, apparently someone forgot because somebody slipped; the birthday boy himself actually. He slipped. Well not so much slipped but rather boldly declared to Peter, one of the Petroski boys, that he turns 5 tomorrow. I would have guessed a different culprit, but as dinner prep is taking place later on Debbie says "I heard someone has a birthday tomorrow." Busted. "Yes," I confess, "my son, Alexander, turns 5 tomorrow."

My future farmer.

"We'll have to make a cake for him," she replies, her daughter Sarah nodding her head in agreement in the background, "and maybe make a special dinner. What is his favorite meal?"

Trying to convince them that it is not necessary to go to such trouble is futile and I finally concede. "He loves macaroni and cheese," I inform them.

"Well, that's easy. Great. And what about the cake? What kind of cake would he like? Does he have a favorite superhero?"

So it's set. A simple chocolate cake with white icing and a Robin (from Batman and Robin) action figure would follow a Mac N Cheese dinner. Sarah is apparently quite the artist as well as the family baker so she is quite eager to get working on the cake.

In the morning I have my phone/camera in ready position for the moment Alexander wakes up. The moment I see the whites of his eyes I click a picture of his smiling face as I whisper, "Happy birth-day my 5 year old." He gives me his grin of embarrassment, but I know he loves the attention. The annual birthday interview will have to wait until later.

Each birthday I interview the birthday boy or girl on video for future blackmail -- err, for future memories. There is a list of standard questions I run through in addition to some personalized question depending on the age and the child. They **LOVE** their birthday interviews and usually insist we do it the moment they wake up. I've tried that, but usually their zeal exceeds their lucidity and the interview goes best after they have been awake for a bit.

After breakfast, we make our way to downtown San Antonio. Deb-bie sends us off with peanut butter and jelly sandwiches on home-made bread along with some snacks for an easy and inexpensive lunch. Can't visit San Antonio and not visit the Alamo, so off we go to relive history.

We park downtown in a lot. I'm a bit irked that I had to pay 10 bucks to park and even more irked when I see a parking lot closer to downtown and half the price as we walk from the car to the Alamo. "Oh well," I muse to myself, trying to talk myself out of the impending funk before it sets in, "it's just a few bucks and we are going to have a good time."

I'm not sure what I expected San Antonio to look like but it's been so built up in my mind I just hope I'm not left disappointed. It's Saturday and the crowds are already gathering. I didn't really think this through. I don't like crowds or cities in general, yet somehow I managed to plan a day at a major tourist attraction on a Saturday when the crowds are bound to be in full force. "We're going to have fun," I tell myself again.

We find our way to the Alamo - or at least to the line already forming to get into the Alamo - just as two little boys state they need to go potty. I suppose better to go now than to rush through the site with a potty emergency. So we weave through the line and find our way inside the mall along the riverfront and into a bathroom. Once all is well we exit the mall. As soon as we step outside the girls see the river itself and the touristy boats lining up to give tours.

"Mom, can we go on a boat?" asks one. "Yeah mom, can we go on that boat?" echoes another in full support. "We'll see. Let's go check out the prices," comes my informed reply. I am not about to repeat the mistake I made in Little Rock when I agreed to something before knowing the actual cost.

I'm not a cheapskate, usually. And especially on this trip I gave myself a pep talk about being willing to spend money and create memories. Free is better, but I wasn't about to take this epic trip and deny us the opportunity to experience some amazing things solely because Mom is being an unnecessary tightwad. However, I'm not keen on paying inflated prices for lackluster experiences. Specifically in relation to these boats, if the price is not worth the length of the ride, it is going to be a big fat no.

As we get to the ticket window all four of them are in agreement that a boat ride is a fantastic idea. The price is reasonable and it is a decent length of a ride, so all aboard we go. The kids are thrilled to just be on a boat and I'm pleasantly surprised to discover that our boat master (or whatever they are called) not only ensures that we don't crash or sink, but also narrates for us as we go, giving us history about the river walk itself. I find it all interesting at the time, but sadly the only detail I remember now is the spot where Sandra Bullock's character in Miss Congeniality 2 jumps off the stage at a Texan carrying (as if that needed to be stated - don't all Texans carry?) thinking the fella was going to shoot someone.

Anyway, when we arrive back to the starting point it seems a good time to head back to the Alamo. After all, when people hear that we went to San Antonio they will inevitably ask, "Did you see the Alamo?" We head back to the entrance but this time don't get anywhere near the entrance. What was a rather short line has grown tremendously. A potty break that should have been handled before we left the house, which led to a boat detour, now has us in a ridiculously long line. So what's a mother to do? Torture her kids by making them stand in the very long line for a site of which they are probably too young to grasp its significance? Why, yes, of course! We came to San Antonio to visit the Alamo and visit the Alamo we shall.

My girls in Austin, TX sporting their new skirt & dress.

The line is actually moving at a decent pace and once we get inside I realize why. Everyone is shuffling through almost like robots, moving from display to display at a most unnatural rate. You cannot possibly absorb much of anything between the crowd and the pace. I suppose I could slow down, but then I'd be "that slow person" and my kids just want out of here anyway. And by now I do as well. There are way too many people in way too small a space. So as quickly as we entered we also exit.

I do not recall a single thing about the Alamo other than its color (white, I think) and the general story, which I knew before arriving. But, when someone hears that we visited San Antonio and asks the inevitable question I can answer in full honesty, "Yes, we did visit the Alamo. We even went inside." Mission accomplished.

All that standing in line makes one hungry so we find a place to sit, eat and conduct the birthday interview. Alexander is a hoot. Both what he says and what he doesn't say crack me up. I cannot wait until each of them comes of age, or maybe on the eve of their wedding, when I present to them the collection of birthday interviews from each year of life. To watch how they grow physically and see how they think from year to year and how their interests change (or don't change), all of that will be a wonderful gift to them and a wonderful memory for me.

For now, however, we head back to the car for the 45 minute drive back to the house. It's only mid-afternoon but I can only take so much tourism at a stretch. Hopefully the Petroski's don't mind an early return.

When we arrive the kids are as fast as ever in finding their new playmates. I step into the kitchen to see a remarkable sight. "We looked for a Robin cake topper, but couldn't find one. They had Batman, but no Robin," Debbie offers apologetically, "so Sarah had to do this."

"This is amazing," I say in reply. "No apology is needed." Instead of a cheap, made-in-China figurine that would be broken within moments there is a hand crafted picture of Robin being created before my eyes. "You are amazingly talented," I tell Sarah in all sincerity. "Have you had lessons or is your talent pure gifting?"

Sarah is clearly too embarrassed and/or humble to reply, but Debbie has no problem chiming in. "She hasn't had any lessons, it's innate talent," she tells me as she reaches for a few sketches Sarah has done. "Unbelievable," I say, feeling like I'm repeating myself but in total awe of her skill, "you are tremendously gifted." Sarah offers a faint and embarrassed, "thank you" to all of my gushing. "Alexander is going to love this! Please let me know when it is done because I definitely want a picture of this before it gets cut."

At dinnertime, we sit down to the mac n' cheese feast that Debbie and Sarah so kindly prepared. Much to my surprise Debbie also brings out a balloon for Alexander. The good kind of balloon. The ones I am too cheap to buy. The kind you find in the grocery store and, if your kids are anything like mine, the kind they ask you to buy because on it they recognize their favorite character. Alexander's eyes just light up. Debbie ties it on the back of his chair as if he is the king, and I suspect right now he feels like a king. Watching his delight over a relatively simple meal and a single balloon creates such a joy in my own heart, and such gratefulness. This family didn't know us yesterday but they have gone out of their way to make this day special for my son.

When the time comes for cake, he is beyond thrilled as he looks at the Robin figure, which appears to be in mid-jump. There are few things that bring me more joy that watching the authentic joy that rouses in my children. This is most certainly one of those times. As if a special meal, a balloon and a cake weren't enough Debbie presents Alexander with a gift. He opens it in record time and offers his sweet, hearty "thank you" as he marvels at his new set of five matchbox cars. Five. V. 5 whole cars - just for him. He cannot believe it, and neither can I. The kindness and genuine hospitality from folks who were strangers 24 hours ago is overwhelming.

Future Dreams and Current Sacrifices

April 6

We are on a roll now. Second Sunday in a row that we will actually attend church. And the first time in a while that I've been excited to attend church. For the most part on this trip it's been drudgery - partly because of the inevitable small talk, partly because of the amount of energy required to get us all ready and then monitor behavior while in church. But whatever church this family attends it must be great, so I am eager to go.

Debbie seems a bit nervous and preps me: "It's a *very* small congregation." She emphasizes very. "And we don't agree with them on everything, but they are faithful believers."

It is very small indeed, but the service is Christ exalting and the sermon is solid. After the service we share a fellowship meal. I love this concept and we have partaken in a few such meals on our journey, usually at the insistence of the Pastor who invites us to stay "if nothing else, to get some lunch before you head on your way." Sunday is usually chaotic to one degree or another, for us at least. And Monday - Saturday isn't always better.

Life is busy and from my experience over the last 11 years as a Christian, authentic fellowship seems rather absent. Oh, we are masters of the fake Sunday smile, the "How are you today?" and the equally rehearsed answer, "I'm great. How are you?" I'll assume the best and say we do truly want to know how others are doing, but how much can you really say as you cross paths from one hallway to the next? And then the service is over, kids are retrieved and out everyone goes.

But the fellowship meal removes the excuse of needing to get home to make lunch. Lunch is right here. Now sit down, relax and visit with someone. Talk to a friend you haven't seen in a while because life is indeed busy. Seek out that older woman from whom you are in desperate need of Titus 2 counsel or, conversely, seek out that new mom with the dazed look clearly needing some encouragement. There is no rush. No hurry. Enjoy yourself. Take your time. Let your children play. And enjoy fellowship with the body of Christ.

Eventually it is time for us to go and I begin to round up my crew. As I step outside to check on my son, who joined the boys in basketball, I see one of the church elders inspecting my car, or at least it seems that way. It is rather odd. Not suspicious, but odd. I walk over, say hello and we begin to exchange pleasantries. There seems to be something on his mind other than the standard formalities but I can't figure out what. Then he shuffles from side to side and says, "I don't know anything about your situation but I think God wants me to give you this." I look down and see a $100 bill in his outstretched hand.

I stare at it for a moment before responding or moving. Finally my brain catches up with the visual and my first thought is to decline. But instead I reach out my hand to accept the gift, look at him and say, "Thank you. That is so very kind of you. I have a hard time accepting kindness from others but one of the things the Lord has taught me over the past few years is to simply say, 'thank you' when someone offers help in any way and receive it. So thank you, truly."

We exchange a few more pleasantries before I say I need to find my children and we need to be on our way. He wishes us all the best and says he will be praying for us. I still don't know if Debbie or John shared anything with him about us. or maybe the sight of a woman traveling on her own with four children was all he needed to know to conclude that we might be in need of help. Either way, I thank my Lord for working in this man and I thank this man for obeying when he felt called to do something.

I eventually locate each of my children and manage to collect them into one place at the same time. If you have more than one child you know what I mean. If not, just wait. I direct them towards the car as I detour to say goodbye to Debbie. She walks us out. The visit that began with an awkward question about my husband is ending way too soon, for me and for her.

Aside from my longtime friend, Angela, this was the first time I offered an expanded explanation for our travels and the back-story to go along with it. In doing so, much to my surprise, I learned that the Petroski family has had their own trials and struggles. Debbie's transparency put to rest my assumption that everyone except me has it all together. The Lord appoints various trials at various times to each of us in order to make us more like Christ. The details of our families are very different, but we both understand hardship, trial and pain. And I know that I am going to miss this woman and her children.

As we say our goodbyes Debbie thrust two $20s into my hand and in a swift slew of words says, "It's not much but we want you to have this. You are doing such a wonderful job with your children and we applaud you for your commitment to homeschool despite everything going on. Please take it." Having just finished the encounter with the elder I was ready for a more graceful response. "I will take it, Debbie. Thank you. It means more than you know." (It meant more than I knew at the time as well).

With that we drive away and I am left thinking for the first time, "This could be the place." All along our journey I have had a keen eye open for where we might settle. Returning to NY has always been out of the question, so the question remains, "where to?" Up to this point nothing has stuck out in my mind as particularly

My little cowboys.

wonderful. The top priority is finding a church, but there is also the practical side of life. I need an income.

Child support will not fully support us and my current job will eventually come to an end. It was never meant to be a remote position. My boss knows I'm traveling, but she assumes it's temporary and that we will be returning to NY in a reasonable amount of time. She has no idea that we have been displaced and are traveling around like vagabonds hoping to find somewhere to settle. There will come a time when I will have to inform her that I am not returning to NY and in all likelihood the job will come to an end when I do. So I need a way to earn income that will be enough to support us, but also allow me to keep my priorities of God first and children second.

As we head west, I consider all that we saw this past weekend: the area itself, the Petroski family, and their circle of likeminded friends we had the privilege of meeting our first night in town. "Lord, is this where you are calling us? Will we become Texans?" Time will tell but for now we head west to an unidentified address.

An excerpt from our email correspondence to arrange this stay went something like this:

Ron: We look forward to having y'all stay. See you Sunday.

Me: Great, thanks so much. I just need an address to plug into my phone.

Ron: Even if I knew my address I don't think your G.P.S. would. Here are the coordinates of where we are...

Abigail loving her first horse ride!

I didn't even reply to that email. What are we getting into here?

By this time on the journey excitement far exceeds hesitancy as we travel from house to house. I am nothing short of eager to meet the next family and learn about them. There has been a lesson for me at each of our stays: whether a practical skill such as sewing a dress or the sight of 12 children happily playing various board games or playing instruments after dinner without a single plea for media and without a single glance an iPhone or an iPad or some other electronic device.

At some homes it has been the encouragement of seeing dad lead family devotions or *how* he leads them as personalities show through. Each family is certainly unique and has different quirks, skills and interests. It's been so interesting to see the different ways different families do family worship, and you can be sure that I've been taking notes.

So while the location of the Evans home is a mystery, it's with eager anticipation that we continue on.

The lack of an address along with intermittent cell service makes this arrival all the more interesting. The closer we get to their town the more rural the scenery becomes. With the rural scenery we may have acheived a record day for animal sightings. I was smart enough to take a screen shot of their location before we left so that with or without cell service I would have a visual.

Annabella at Texas ranch. First horse ride.

We finally turn onto their street and now the fun really begins.

"Okay, Abigail, I think it's this one," gesturing to the right, "but that is quite the driveway. Let's be sure before we turn in because if we are wrong, after the mile long driveway, who knows if we'll be welcomed with shotguns pointed at us."

"Why would they point guns at us, Mom?" she asks wide-eyed. "I don't know for sure but we are in Texas, in rural Texas. Folks may not want strangers on their property and I don't want to take any chances, so let's go a bit further down just make sure."

We drive down a little ways, counting the driveways and comparing our observations to the picture on my phone. Not that there are many driveways to count. All of two. So in reality it's not brain surgery, but that long driveway is intimidating.

It is time to make a decision and commit, so in we turn. As we bump, jostle and jolt our way down the driveway my awe of the home that looked massive from the road becomes even more impressive. We pull up along side a smaller building to the left and as I

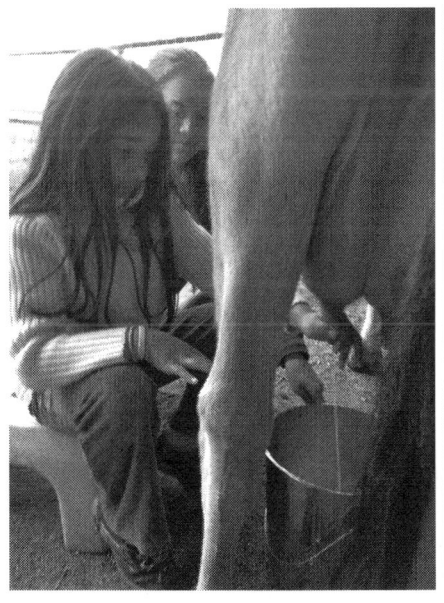
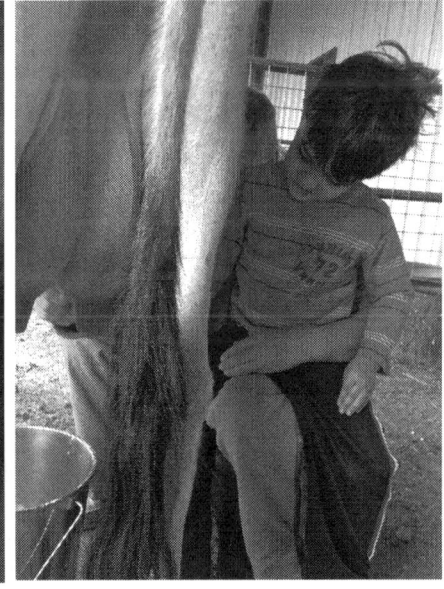

Abigail milking a cow in TX. She was more adventurous than the rest.

Alexander isn't as sure about this.

glance at the home on the right I see a large "E" on the side of the house – "oh yes, this must be the place." Within moments there are two children, bright eyed and wide smiled on bikes. The boy donning a cowboy confirms that we are indeed at the right house.

(The visit to the Evans home was entirely too short. It was an overnighter but we felt like we could have stayed for weeks -- don't know how the Evans' would have felt about that however.)

The bunkhouse where we will be staying is so much more than the name portrays. In my mind I hear bunkhouse and I picture an old barn. In this case bunkhouse means two full bathrooms, two warmly and quaintly decorated guestrooms, a full kitchen, a large main room with two sets of bunk beds on opposite sides and a pool table in the middle. On the side table adjacent the door stands a bowl of fruit and a note welcoming us to their home.

As we explore the bunkhouse to determine where everyone will sleep I can't help but ponder, *this is bigger than any house I might possibly own in the future.* It feels huge, and wonderful and so very welcoming. And was an intentional addition to their property, as I will soon learn.

Darla had told us to get settled and head over whenever we were ready. So after I pick my jaw up off of the floor and finish planning out sleeping arrangements we head over. Crossing the 150 ft between the bunkhouse and the main house I gaze to the left and to the right in awe of the giant sky and seemingly endless land before me. (I'll do the same thing again in the morning while I bask in the beauty of God's creation as the sun creeps over the horizon).

We climb what seems to be an extra high staircase that leads to the main entrance of the house. The impressive stonework outside is just a foretaste of what we will see inside. Entering the house feels like entering a different world. It is a lively home, yet organized. Jovial children yet not obnoxiously loud. This definitely feels like a haven from the world, add to that its distance from anything resembling a town and I am envious.

Darla and some of her girls are in the kitchen preparing dinner, which includes not *just* grass-fed beef, but their own grass-fed beef.

So far the Evans' are living up to my stereotypical image of a Texas ranch family, although I haven't seen any shot guns…yet.

We are welcomed in like old friends and laughter and conversation flows freely. My children find great fun amongst their tribe of ten. From the oldest to the youngest they are sweet respectful children. It is a house very much under control - in the best of ways, not the worst. Peaceful and joyous is the tone; nothing like the potential unruly chaos that could very quickly happen with so many people under one roof. A testimony, I think, to Ron and Darla themselves and the way they have trained up their children.

If it's furry Annabella will try to pick it up!

As Darla sits to chat, I resist the urge to grill her -- she seems to be living a lifestyle that I have long envisioned and I want the facts, the details, and the ten-step plan to get there. Instead, with some semblance of manners I ask one simple question that would lead to all the things I want to know and provide a reality check at the same time.

"How long have you been here?"

In my head, in the fairytale I have written for them, they've been here since their oldest was a baby. In my fairy tale, this house is the only house their children have ever known and every evening Ron and Darla take a moonlight walk hand in hand while their children sleep soundly in their beds. I just met these folks less than two hours ago and I have already written what I think should be their story. But Darla unknowingly shows me that first impressions are not always accurate.

This is a truth I have already encountered on this trip and will encounter a few more times. First impressions, whether positive or negative, are rarely the whole story. By now I should be more adept at keeping my assumptions in check, but I can't seem to help grasping at the idea that someone else's life can indeed be a fairy tale story. And then, if that fairy tale is true for them, it could be true for me.

In reality, no life is without pain and hardship. No success, however that is measured, is without sacrifice. It's not about avoiding the rainstorms all together but to borrow and old cliché, it's about singing in the rain.

Ron and Darla bought this property over ten years ago. They wanted a ranch and the ranch life. For the first seven years they lived in a trailer on the property while they saved up for their dream house. Their oldest child is nearly 20, so this was far from the story I had written in my mind. They were married for over ten years before they bought this property and then lived in a way that most people would not be willing to, in order to have their dream. How many folks are willing to delay what they want for any length of time.

Seven years - that's a long time! Seven years of waiting and of living in a sacrificial way so that eventually they *could* have what they want.

One day a buddy of theirs approached them and said, "The old girls' home in town is about to be demolished. Do you want the house?"

They went to look at it and it was in disrepair. It would not be as simple as moving the house from point a to point b and moving in. The structure was solid but everything else was not. Ron was able to look at the edifice and see its potential. They had a foundation laid on their property, moved the house and began work. What I now see is the result of much patience, lots of vision and plenty of sweat equity.

I like Darla's story, the real story, better than the one I constructed. Not that she needs my approval. But for my own sake, it's good to be reminded that life is toil, and that's okay. Am I going to keep a good attitude in the midst of the toil?

Big Bend, TX. A band of exhausted children wanting to know where the promised hot spring is.

The only question left is about the bunkhouse. When and how did that come about? Ron chimed in with a most logical answer and one that reveals their intentionality. "We wanted a guesthouse that we would be comfortable in if we were traveling somewhere; something big enough to fit our whole family. And when grandparents visit we want them to be comfortable and have everything they might need."

How wonderful to have the space to do that. How fantastic to have a set aside guest area where, as my friend Trina Holden says, "extravagant hospitality" can be shown. We certainly feel like royalty in that bunkhouse. We have our own space to sleep, to shower, to play. We don't feel disturbed by their morning routine nor do I worry about us disturbing them. If we were staying for an extended period of time we would be well equipped to prepare our own meals without interfering in their family routine.

*****

We sleep wonderfully well and the cool, crisp morning air is nothing short of refreshing. Thankfully today is a short drive so there is no big hurry to leave. We are able to linger and soak in some more time with the Evans'. So what does one do in the morning on a Texas

The reward for the long hike. Hot spring at last.

ranch? I don't know about the locals but my kids milk a cow, ride a horse and zip on a zip line. It feels like one of those old Army commercials, "We do more before 10am than most people do all day."

A week or so later when I sit down to write a thank you note to Ron and Darla I am sitting in front of my computer instead of a paper and pen. My note starts with: "I sat down to write a quick thank you note and realized I don't have an address to send it to." I expressed my appreciation once again for their hospitality and Ron's response was most gracious and Jesus centered, "You are very welcome. I love how in GOD's world that when we blessed you we were greatly blessed also. We loved meeting you and your family."

How true his words are and how applicable to various aspects of life. God calls us to obedience and then blesses us for obeying. God calls us to hospitality and then blesses us when we do so. God calls us to love others and blesses us when we do. Our God is truly an awesome God!

Miscommunication and The Real Deal

April 9 –

I must admit, when we enter a house that just seems too organized and too clean to be for real I can't help but wonder how much of what I see is their everyday norm and how much of it is part of their preparation for hosting strangers. In some homes it seems quite clear that they did not do any special cleaning for our visit. Other homes I think there is no way that what I see what their house looks like on a regular basis. And it has often been the families that say, "Please ignore the mess" or "Please ignore the lack of cleanliness" and then offer an excuse or two that are usually cleaner and more organized than most. I'm not even sure why I wonder such things other than an attempt to compare myself.

Oh, I'm sure I try to sanctify such thoughts in my mind; excuse it as something other than sinful pride or self-righteousness, but I think the truth is I want to know how I compare. How do I match up? Where do I stand on the scale (a scale I myself created) of house-keeping? But come on, be honest, haven't you wondered, no matter what they said, whether your friend did a massive 15 minute clean before you walked through the door? Did your Pastor's wife throw everything into a closet to hide the children's mess? How much of what you are seeing is authentic life and how much is manufactured for the sake of appearances?

Now, I have nothing wrong with tidying up a home before company arrives. Short of pride or vanity I see no sin in wanting to present hospitality that involves some additional effort. But I do indeed have a secret longing to gain an authentic glimpse at life in another home. I want to know what their norm is for everyday life versus the norm for guests; like the hospitality of decades past when you didn't need to set a time, you didn't need to call ahead, you could just "pop in" and see if so-and-so is home. Well, we are about to find out.

Another day another state. Crossing state lines is now as common as stopping for gas. I made up a silly ritual early on in the trip that only Abigail and I follow. She sits shotgun and is my copilot and loves keeping an eye out for state signs. "Here we go," I shout as we take

Sledding down the sand dunes at
White Sands, NM was a family favorite.

in a deep breath. The "leaving Texas" sign is just ahead. "Whew," we let out the air in a most dramatic fashion. "We're in New Mexico," I gleefully declare. This silly routine always makes her smile and it adds some fun to the monotony of driving.

I have been working two weeks at a time with lining up places to stay. I can't seem to plan much more than two weeks ahead and as a result sometimes it's less than a week when I make a request to stay with a family from the network. Not the best planning, but thus far it has worked. But with this next family I was on the ball; the Stanek's were lined up two full weeks ago. I'm rather proud of my planning this time around.

Our standard arrival time is 4pm. Early enough that the kids can play with other kids, late enough that if the family is really strange we don't have to socialize too long before bedtime. The one glitch is time zones. I usually forget and it throws of the timing. We are already ahead of schedule despite stopping for an oil change, but with the extra hour traveling from CST to MST we are really early.

"It doesn't look like anyone is home. What do you think, are they home?" I ask, not so much to anyone in particular, more like thinking out loud. "Yeah, I don't think they're home. Austin is sleeping, maybe we should drive a bit," I say to whoever might be listening, but mostly to myself as I check my phone.

All of the home stays are lined up via email, which is fantastic, since I dread the phone. While looking for the email record to check the stated arrival time I hear, "but we are here mom, let's just go see." Abigail is eager to get out of the car and stretch her legs. "Huh," I say even more so to myself this time. "What is it?" my Abigail wants to know. "It looks like I never told Mrs. Stanek what time we would arrive. I'm not sure what time she is expecting us." "Can we just go check, Mom?" Abigail asks again. I concede, mostly because I don't anticipate anyone answering, "Alright, you girls can go knock on the door and see if they are home."

The girls bound to the door like racehorses out of the stall and knock. They wait a few more moments and knock again. Finally the door opens and I see a young woman. Clearly they are home; I guess we are getting out.

After a brief conversation with the young woman the girls return to the car. I help Alexander out of the car and pick up Austin, who is still sleeping. I leave the bags for now and we head to the door. Jessica lets us in and a few moments later the matriarch of the family appears. "What's going on?" she asks, appearing not quite fully lucid. "We're here," I reply, not sure if she's joking. "But who are you?" she asks, in all seriousness. "Oh, well, I thought your daughter here knew," I say, quite confused.

Apparently, my girls confirmed they were home but failed to introduce themselves. I guess by now, having visited so many homes with people expecting us, the girls just assumed the person answering the door knew who we where and why we were there -- not necessarily a bad assumption, despite what may have been an absence of manners at the moment. So Jessica let us in not having the slightest clue who we were.

"We are the Amaya's. I had emailed you about staying through the network," I say, hoping that resolves it all. By now I'm feeling very awkward. "Oh yes, I remember that, but that was ages ago and you

White Sands, NM. Cheesy mom

never confirmed with me", Kathy replies, as equally confused as I am. "I thought it was all set. I actually just checked my email to see what time I told you we'd be arriving, I never did. I dropped the ball there. But I thought the visit itself was confirmed." As I'm speaking my mind is problem solving. Don't I feel dumb. We'll go find a hotel I guess. No big deal.

"That's alright. We're totally unprepared, but if you don't mind we don't mind. Come on in." We are still standing in the entryway having progressed no further in all the confusion. "Are you sure?" I ask in response. "We messed up and I don't want to put you out. We can figure something else out, it's really alright." "No, I dropped the ball," says Kathy. "You confirmed and I forgot. Come on in already, ignore the mess, this is life, but come in."

Once we all get passed the shock of the situation it becomes an ongoing joke over the next two days.

Kathy calls her husband John and asks him to hit up Costco on the way home. "We have visitors. I totally forgot, John, but they are here and we need food." What a man he must be. Strangers he wasn't even expecting are in his house and apparently it's a-okay with him.

"You know, you really missed out," Kathy says with a smile. "We usually have a guest basket all set up in the room when our guests come. I don't have any of that for you. You'll have to come again another time when we can be properly prepared." As she speaks she is navigating the living room, around the various toys and animals strewn about and once again asks me to ignore the mess.

"Oh, I love it," I say enthusiastically, "you didn't have time to prepare for us and now we get to see how you really live. None of the facade, just reality."

Now Kathy is not what I'd call a young mother. Jessica, her daughter, is a decade younger than me and is the youngest of the four biological children. Out back with my crew are two girls and a boy, ages 7, 3 and 3 (twins). Sound like a unique line-up? It truly is. Kathy and John had four biological children in the normal course of marriage. Three are now married and out of the home. Jessica is not yet married and has chosen to remain at home to help mom and dad with the young ones.

At an age in life when most people are ready to enjoy the "empty nest" and delight in the "golden years", ready to kick back, retire and live out the rest of their years in leisure, John and Kathy asked, "What should we do now?" Instead of the "normal" response, theirs was, "Let's adopt." And adopt they did. Three young children, whom Kathy also homeschools.

As I sit and listen to Kathy tell the story, it's clear she is unaware of how uncommon their choices are and she is completely unimpressed by their sacrifices. But I'm impressed. And I marvel. Marvel at an amazing God who put it in their heart and is enabling them to carry out this vision. Marvel that these two people who have "earned the right" (as many would say) to simply enjoy life, have instead devoted their lives once again to the nurture and admonition of children. I marvel at the picture that adoption always shows us of Christ adopting us and calling us His own.

I also marvel at the priorities of Jessica, who is also going against the grain, not only of culture at large, but also of Christian culture. At the "prime of her life" she *should be* out there, making a name for herself, pursuing a career, partying with friends, and the like. Instead she is giving back to her parents by helping raise her younger siblings. She is putting self aside to further God's kingdom in the lives of these little ones.

No, she is neither socially awkward nor isolated. She is a wonderful conversationalist, quite fashionable, as if I have any fashion sense, and very smart. She pursues her own particular interests while she develops the various skills God has given her, including cultivating her homemaking skills with the hope that one day she too will have a husband and children to care for.

Detours

April 13

We just left Rio Rancho. It's been a great time with the Jaslow family. They aren't even a part of the hospitality network. The Jones' in Missouri used to live in New Mexico and when I told Peter and Jennifer of our plans to visit this area they not only gave us locations worth visiting, but also connected us to their good friends, the Jaslows, so we would have somewhere to stay.

My Bandelier gang. NM

Today, we are heading west and as we do the stress of all the uncertainty is weighing on me once again. Not that the stress ever fully goes away. I merely feel varying degrees of stress - and today it is at the higher end. The constant cycle of lining up house stays is wearing me out. In a week we will be in California visiting my brother and his wife. While I am not looking forward to the hotel bill that will come with the California visit, I am looking forward to having a few days that will hopefully feel like downtime. And I still need to determine just how much time we can spend in California. My brother's studio apartment simply does not have room for five additional people so however long we are on the west coast we will be in a hotel.

*****

I distinctly remember my fourth grade history textbook. Well, not all of it. Not most of it, actually. I remember one picture from my fourth grade history textbook - the four corners. To 10-year old me it seemed a magical place. It was a picture taken from the sky pointed directly at the ground at the exact point that Colorado, Utah, New Mexico and Arizona meet - 4 states hence 4 corners. In the photo, the place where they all met was gray, as if made of stone. Lines were etched into the ground denoting the exact location where Utah began and Colorado ended; each section having the respective state name boldly etched into it.

My 10-year old brain thought it must be the coolest place ever and since then I've had an infatuation with this mystical, magical place. Today, I will fulfill the lifelong dream to visit these four corners and, like at so many of our trip destinations, check off another bucket list item.

Now I did my research a few weeks ago while sick in bed in Tennessee - which in itself is impressive, since I'm more of a fly-by-the-seat-of-my-pants type of person when it comes to traveling. I tend to assume that I know where I'm going and that my getting-lost-radar somehow turned itself off. But this time I wasn't taking any chances.

I had directions written out. I researched the corners on various travel forums – "visit a bathroom before you get there, unless you don't mind a port-o-john, and come with anything you might need. There is nothing for miles. Rugged." With this feedback in mind we stop at a grocery store, put together a packed lunch and with my kids completely clueless to today's agenda, we head out to picnic in this magical place.

Oh, it's all planned out. The photos are already choreographed in my mind. I've got 4 kids and there are 4 states to cover. Bam! One kid in each corner. Then we'll rotate around one by one until each has set foot in all four states. Then we'll do the "one foot in one state, the other foot in another state" pose. Then I'll have them lie down, each in a different state, their heads meeting in the middle. Then each kid sprawled out over all 4 states. It is going to be a blast. A hoot. A fantastic time.

This fantastic time is sure costing us time. It is an hour detour on the way to it and thereby another hour will be added to our trip after leaving. So in all, living out this childhood fantasy would cost us two hours. But I'm convinced it will be totally worth it.

As we near the location the sky begins to get dark. Very, very dark. I drive faster and tell the kids, "Listen, a storm is coming. When we get there we are all going to run. You *WILL* cooperate for a few pictures and we'll get back in the car before the rain comes. Got it?"

We make the left hand turn into the site and I see a booth. As we near the booth I see a sign, "Entry Fee $10." What in the world? So much for desolate. I guess the Navajo have decided to cash in on the tourism. I don't blame them but neither am I too pleased. I begrudgingly pay my $10 just as the first few raindrops fall on my windshield.

Pulling into the parking lot it looks nothing like the descriptions I've read nor the pictures I've seen in my research. There are booths set up where other Navajo are selling various items. Instead of an isolated stone marking each of the states there is a rather elaborate display area. But all of that is simply distracting me from the task at hand. In the 15 seconds it takes to pay the entry fee and park the car the skies open and the rain comes a tumbling down. It is pouring and the wind is gushing.

I attempt to open my door but the wind fights back and pushes it closed. My kids, who weren't all that enthused about helping mom live out this childhood fantasy to begin with and saw absolutely no excitement about a rock in the ground, are now even less eager to step out into this storm and stand around for mom to take pictures.

"Come on guys. Real quick," I say. I jump out, open the passenger door behind me and begin to get the boys out of their seats. Seeing them stand there, rain dripping down their faces as they feebly try to shield themselves from the onslaught of attacking water reminds me that I'm a mom first, a tourist second. "Get back in," I shout over the cacophony of rain and wind blowing. The girls have barely stepped outside; they simply reverse their process and cheerfully close their door.

I get the boys loaded back into their seats and climb back into my own. As I look at the rain, which is about all I can look at - it is raining so hard I can't see much past my windshield, I evaluate: *I've driven two hours out of the way to come here. It's doubtful I'll ever*

2 hour detour for this picture

come here again because it is so out of the way. I've always wanted to visit. We are here now. That's it, I want my picture.

"Stay here, I'll be right back," I declare with the bravado one would expect from a military hero about to do something courageous, "I want my photograph." Before they can even respond I push open the door, throw on my hood and run as fast as I can to the monument. I run up the Arizona ramp to get a slightly elevated view, take out my camera, point and shoot. Trusting that the camera is at least aimed in the right direction I tuck it back into my pocket for protection, turn and make a b-line back to the car. Soaking wet I slip back into my seat and just sit. Content to have a picture, but annoyed that my perfectly planned outing has literally been rained upon, I start the car and we drive away.

"Oh well", I console myself, "in ten years I really won't care much about not seeing four corners better, and I'll have quite a story for my future grandkids."

Less than 10 minutes later,the skies clear and the sun comes out.

Grand Canyon – colder than we expected

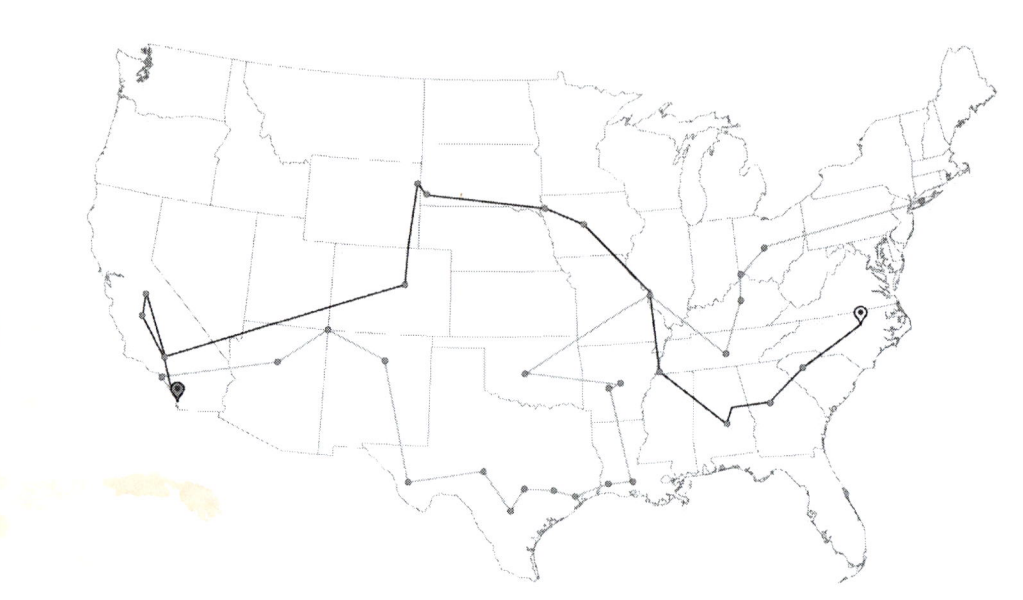

Part Two

A Glimmer of Hope

New Beginnings

April 20 –

Easter in California. We head over to Jimmy and Lauren's apartment after church where Lauren has a small egg hunt prepared for the kids. Jimmy got the "laid back" genes in the family so little is scheduled and the day is *very* loosely planned - whatever plans do exist, I'm fairly certain I can thank Lauren. It's actually quite nice to have a relaxed holiday. I don't know that this particular day has much significance for either of them aside from tradition, but the kids and I enjoyed a good church service and it's a relief to have nothing required for the rest of the day.

After the egg hunt, Lauren takes the girls for a special girl treat: manicures and pedicures. For having a tom-boy mama, these girls are as girly as they come, and I love it. The boys head out for some guy time in the form of lacrosse. Jimmy is a coach and my boys have taken a liking to the sport - mostly, I suspect, because Uncle Jimmy is teaching them. That leaves me free to do...whatever. I

Time with Uncle Jimmy

know my kids feel like kings and queens with their activities, but I'm convinced I received the best gift - alone time! After well over six weeks of being with my children every second of every day it feels amazing to drive the car by myself, park the car by myself, get out of the car without waiting for anyone, and walk into a store without constantly scanning to make sure I don't lose anyone.

Now what would one do with total free time? Well, I head to the nearby Whole Foods to enjoy lunch from their buffet bar. I sit outside with a book, enjoying the sun and the quiet as I eat. I get up and go for a walk at my own pace. I walk back to my car and drive over to the self-serve car wash down the road for a very long over-due car cleaning. It takes two wash cycles. I vacuum the six-weeks worth of dirt, garbage and snacks that have accumulated. I stand back and admire my work.

A few hours of childlessness is enjoyable, refreshing and takes some getting used to. A toddler calls "mommy" in a store and I instinc-tively turn. Oh right, that's not my child. It certainly gives me time to think without interruption. And there is plenty to think about. Thus far my story has been, "We are heading to California to visit my brother and sister-in-law." Now we are here. Under normal circumstances logic would dictate that we begin our return to New York continuing to sightsee on the way. But there is no return. New York is not our destination. We don't have a destination. So now what? I once again find myself calling out to the Lord for wisdom and direction.

One of the goals I have for this trip, aside from survival, is to figure out where we want to be. San Antonio is a possibility, but even there I don't see anything definitive. There is no clear-cut path. We have now made it to the opposite coast and I still don't have a plan.

The top priority is settling down in a theologically solid church. Now, more than ever, I am aware of the importance of a local church. A church where men act like men and lead like biblical men. Where they come along side a family like mine, providing biblical council for the numerous decisions and tough situations we will inevitably face. Willing and able to help fill the role left by an absent husband and father. .Offering practical help, including mentorship for my boys.

Despite what feminism says both inside and outside of the church, men are needed. They are irreplaceable. Women as wives and mothers cannot fulfill the role of husband and father. By God's grace, children raised in broken homes can still grow up to love and serve Him. By God's grace these children of mine are not doomed to be a statistic of violent criminals and delinquents. But it is still far from ideal. I never wanted this, for them or for me. But this is our lot in life and I simply cannot teach my boys how to be men. I cannot provide the guidance and instruction a father is meant to pass on to his sons. Nor can I fill the role of father in my daughters' lives. I need a church where there are men who first and foremost are discipling their own children and secondly are sensitive to the children in the congregation that are missing that discipleship and are ready, willing and able to step in and help.

Finding such a church is no small order - where in the world do I begin? That is a question I start asking the Lord with great urgency.

Job Hunts

April 21 –

I need to accept the possibility that my future may involve a job outside the home - maybe full time, maybe part time. It may require kids in school rather than homeschooled. I've already had one job interview during our travels and need to be ready for more.

While at the Creation Museum in Petersburg, KY at the outset of our trip I had scanned their display of flyers and brochures. Abigail zeroed in on the card for a cave exploring expedition with Buddy Davis. "Abigail, we can't do that, Austin just isn't old enough yet to even consider it," was not the response she wanted. The boys were amused by anything with a dinosaur on it. Annabella grabbed one of just about everything -- my little collector and hoarder. The sole flyer that caught my eye said, "Creation Museum is hiring."

"Well, if full time work is in my future, what better place for me and for them than to be influenced by the Creation Museum," I had told myself as I placed the flyer in my bag.

Several weeks later, the museum had responded to my inquiry for a nighttime housekeeping position and I had a phone interview with the HR manager while my children were taking their first horse rides down in Texas. I wasn't offered the position, so we won't be heading out to Kentucky anytime soon, but I still need to pursue the possibility of working. At the same time, I still cannot embrace the possibility of leaving my babies every day to go off to some job.

My kids are so much more valuable than any income I could ever make. I quit my $72,000 a year job 8 years ago to be at home with Abigail - a decision I never for a second regretted. Now I'm applying to $10 an hour part-time positions at Costco, Whole Foods and Ikea. But if that is what it will take to care for my babies then that's what I'll do. At least with a part time position I'll still be home a bit and maybe can even continue to homeschool.

Where are the men?

April 23

We are loaded up and heading north. Last night we attended Jimmy's lacrosse game at the school where he coaches. He sent the boys off with their own lacrosse sticks - a belated birthday gift for Alexander and an early one for Austin. Today Austin turns 3.

After we eat breakfast our first stop is Bellflower, CA for a taping of The Comfort Zone at Living Waters ministry. We tried to see a taping last Friday, but it was cancelled last minute, much to our collective disappointment. Thankfully we have to drive right past that town today anyway, so it works out perfectly.

My kids have no clue who any of the current pop stars or famous actors are (neither do I really), but the hosts of The Comfort Zone -- Ray, EZ and Mark -- they know. My kids have sat through many-a show while sitting on our couch, laptop propped open on the table in front of us. But now they get to see them live and in person. Meeting these three men covers more than half of the "famous" people in my kid's world. *For inquiring minds, the other two "celebrities" my crew recognizes is Todd Friel of Wretched Radio and Caleb Holt aka Kirk Cameron, from Fireproof.*

We arrive fifteen minutes early for taping, as requested. I give my kids the standard threatening lecture before we go in: "We are here because everyone wanted to see the show. I'm excited to be here and they are kind enough to let us come. You WILL sit still and you must be quiet. I know you can behave and I expect you to do so." It doesn't matter how excited a child might be before an event, all bets are off at the event. You just never know.

We are escorted into the studio where the men are already sitting down and the crew is making last minute adjustments. I have followed this ministry ever since the Lord saved me in 2002 after listening to two of Ray's sermons. I am very familiar with their work and have many of their resources. It's easy to feel like I know each of them personally, but I forget that we are total strangers to them. They know nothing about us.

The standard greetings are given. They introduce themselves, as if we needed the introduction, and ask if we have ever seen the show. "Yes, many times." I reply. "You guys are celebrities in our house."

Mark has five pint sized water bottles on his desk, one for each of us, and Ray wins their affection with candy. "You do want them quiet, right?" I ask, lightheartedly. They all laugh. I even made the "funny guy" laugh. The funny guy - Alexander's nickname for EZ. "He always does funny things," as Abigail explains. The taping soon starts and I shoot up a prayer that my kids would stay quiet and not ruin the taping.

Thirty minutes of taping flies by and the kids are mesmerized the whole time. They spend the thirty minutes shifting their gaze from the three people in front of us to the three faces on the TV screen above Mark's head and back down to the live people once again. Mark seems to take every possible opportunity to make faces at the kids or otherwise try to make them laugh. It seems my fear of a child breaking the perfect silence on set is unfounded both because they do just fine and because it is very much a lighthearted environment.

We sat in on a taping of The Comfort Zone

When it is all over EZ asks where we are from. As soon as I say New York Ray immediately chimes in and asks quite seriously, with his New Zealand accent, "You are traveling all that way without your husband or another man with you, and with four children? Are you quite safe?" It's a question I have heard before stated one way or another and I'm quite comfortable answering it.

"My husband left us two years ago and we are on our own. We are out in California visiting my brother."

He isn't satisfied, "Don't you have a church to look after you? Elders?"

Now that response I am not ready for. The directness takes me by surprise and I'm relieved when I see all three men seemingly in a rush as they quickly gather their things -- I am at a loss for words - I have no reply.

He is right though. He is 100% right. Where is the church to look after us and elders to care for us? Why am I traveling all this way, on my own, with four children?

Whether Ray sees this adventure as irresponsible on my part or on the part of the church or both, I don't know, but I can't imagine his response if he knew the whole truth. What would he say if he knew we are traveling because we have to – because we have no home?

Mark and EZ head out the back door of the studio with Ray following. Before he fully exits, Ray turns and says to meet him in the front, he has something for the kids. We are escorted through the door we entered and back to the reception area. While we wait for what seems to be an unnecessarily long time the kids keep busy looking at the books in the bookstore and wondering if the wax fruit on the table is real.

Eventually Ray emerges with a small teddy bear for each of my kids (Alexander later names his bear "Ray Comfort") and hands me one of his books, *God Speaks*. I read the subtitle as we head out the side door to our car, *Finding Hope in the Midst of Hopelessness* and I'm left to ponder Ray's words, "Don't you have a church to look after you? Elders?"

Light at the End of the Tunnel?

April 25

Clarity often comes after complete desperation leads me to my knees. "What now?" has been a question asked multiple times over the last few days. From immediate issues like, "where do we go after California - do we head north or back east?" to the overarching question that has been asked since we left on March 6 – "What's the end game, Lord?" With that question comes an assumption that there is an end other than forever being nomads. I know that this world is not our home. I know we are all travelers and I have felt very much like an Israelite traveling through the desert over the past few years - nothing certain, constantly moving, desperately aware of my moment-by-moment dependence upon the Lord. "Give us *this day*" takes on a whole new meaning when one truly doesn't know what tomorrow will bring.

Birthday Boy! Austin turns 3

Last night it occurred to me that we live in a digital age. I've been asking the question, "How to find a church?" all the while forgetting that the internet is at my disposal. Anytime I need an answer to a question or need a resource to solve a problem I Google it. Why hadn't I thought of this already?

Ordinarily, I have been going to sleep at the same time as the kids. Partly because we have almost always been in the same room and I don't want to keep them up. But also because I can use the extra sleep. Stress can and is taking its toll on me and sleeping more than I normally would is keeping me somewhat sane. But after the kids are in bed this night, I quietly pull out my computer and begin my search. With so many reliable directories out there, surely I can find some leads. But where to begin?

Well, I know there are certain states I prefer due to favorable home-school laws and I don't want to go too far west because if there is any possibility of me keeping my current job I need to be within a day's drive of NYC. After considering potential locations, cross referencing the various directories and taking a close look at church websites I come up with a list of five churches. If only I had thought of this before even leaving NY – I could have potentially saved a lot of time by making a point to visit each of these churches on the way. But I'm here now and at least I have a plan going forward.

With the list of churches I begin sending out an email to each pastor offering a brief overview of our situation and asking if a family like mine might be a fit for their church. I am very much interested in *how* each pastor responds more than *what* specifically they say. Do they seem to make assumptions in their response? Do they make snap decisions without hearing a fuller explanation of everything? Do they present their church like Disneyland, as if it is the happiest place on earth?

I don't wait long to find out. In the morning I have my first response.

The first pastor that responds is from the church that most impressed me initially. But also the church that I quickly discounted after realizing it was in St. Louis, MO. I'm not a city person and I really don't want to be in a city as large as St. Louis. But after further pondering I remind myself that there are suburbs and I need to keep my options open.

I am very impressed with the response from Pastor Seth – he is Gospel centered in his reply and invites us to not only visit the church but also stay with him and his family while we are in the area. A few more exchanges back and forth and for the first time I see a light at the end of the tunnel.

Defining Moment

April 28

"So tell me, what made you decide to take this trip?" That is the question that makes seconds feel like hours.

We arrived at the Howe house in Northern California last night after spending an unforgettable afternoon at Yosemite National Park. They were arriving home after a weekend away and we pulled in less than an hour after them. This was a home that made you feel welcomed and at ease the moment you walked through the door. There was no elaborate greeting, none was needed. It felt more like entering the home of close friends who were glad to see us but don't require formalities. All twelve of the children were friendly and well mannered and there was no lack of conversation. By bedtime, I knew that this visit would seem way too short.

After breakfast this morning, the kids, both mine and theirs, all run off to play in various corners of the house. With a family of 14 you

Sand play at Yosemite.

can imagine it's a decent sized house. The kitchen is large, with an open floor plan and a chef's table in the center. Down three steps and you are at the long dining room table where most meals are eaten. A few yards past the table is the main gathering area. A fireplace to the right is the center point with couches all around. Not sure what else to do, I make my way to one of the couches and watch my boys play on the floor. It is too early to head out for the day's activities so we will linger for a while. Within a few moments Julie makes her way over and sits in a high-backed upholstered chair across from me, holding baby Joshua, their newest addition.

Julie seems to be a person I could talk to all day, but with all of her responsibilities, caring for her house and her children, I wasn't about to presume upon her time in any way. So when she sits down to talk with me I am thrilled. But then it comes.

"Every homeschooler dreams of taking a trip like the one you are taking. So tell me, what made you decide to take this trip?"

The silence was deafening as I argued in my own head about what to say and how much to share. There are so many reasons, yet one root reason. I've always wanted to take a trip like this, but this specific trip wasn't exactly voluntary.

Before I could finish the internal debate I hear myself saying, "Truth is, I'm looking to get out of New York and we are scouting out the country as we go."

North, South, East, West

April 29

Which way from here? We've made it all the way to California, now what? I know we have one definitive destination to hit no matter which route we choose - one way or another we will head back through St. Louis. But there is so much more of the country to see. Do we head Northwest and visit places I know only by photographs: Oregon, Washington and Montana? I've long wanted to visit Yellowstone National Park and Mount St. Helen's. At the same time we are far away from home - well, not that we have a home, but far away from my comfort zone. Even if I wanted to drive straight through to New York, it would take three whole days of nothing but driving. For some reason the thought of that makes me very uneasy and I have an urge to head as far east as quickly as possible. That inclination is backed up when I am unable to line up a single network stay in any of the northwestern states. So east we will head.

Train ride at Yosemite.

We love an adventure. Yosemite, CA.

Zoom Through the Wild West

May 2

For a state with so much to see, we are sure taking the express route. Two full days of nonstop driving takes us from northern California through Nevada, through Utah, to our next home stay in Colorado. We could have taken a slower pace, but there were no network families along the route and I am eager to get to St. Louis, hoping desperately it is the Promised Land we've been waiting for.

After two days of pretending to be rural farmers in Podunk, Colorado we have another long drive to Denver. This time we are staying with another single parent family. There is something refreshing about spending time with a person who knows what you've been through. Thank the Lord for friends that seek to understand and are support-ive, but to have someone who has walked in your shoes and truly knows how you feel is priceless. If our travel schedule wasn't already set for the next two weeks we would stay longer.

Alexander and Austin's first fishing experience.

Annabella got the first catch of the day!

Mount Rushmore, SD

Mother's Day

May 11

Oh, to hide away and wake up tomorrow. It's Mother's Day and the Jefferson's want us to be a part of their Mother's Day activities. We arrived in St. Louis two days ago and despite their welcoming personalities I still feel awkward. This isn't like a network stay and I'm not sure what to expect. I'm waiting for a sign in the sky saying, *THIS IS THE PLACE*. I had enough forethought to reach out to various churches, but now that I'm here I'm not sure what I'm supposed to do.

How do I evaluate this church? How do I evaluate the area? Do I start looking at apartments? If so, what price range? How can I ever really know if we can survive here financially? What if my job situation changes and I can no longer work remotely, which I suspect will happen? I was hoping all of this travel would be coming to an end once we arrived in St. Louis. Instead I just have a different list of questions needing to be answered. Two days in and I'm not any closer to having anything figured out.

Pastor Seth and his wife Sarah invited me to join in the Mother's Day brunch they were holding for Seth's mom and grandma. I thought it would be fine. Holidays have gotten much easier over the last year and sometimes they come and go without much thought on my part. If anything there is a faint sadness that we aren't spending the holiday as a complete family, but nothing like the emotional mess I was the first two years after he left.

I could have been okay today – it's uncomfortable to celebrate Mother's Day with people I only met a few days ago but I think I would have been okay had not Sarah handed me a bag.

She made gifts for her mother-in-law and grandmother-in-law. That's normal and maybe even expected. What wasn't expected was that she also made one for me. I would have been quite content to watch those two ladies open their inter-familial gifts, but to have her hand me one as well, that was too much.

My kids often make me cards; it's sweet and I keep them. But it has been years since I've been given a gift from someone other than my children and what was intended to be a kind gesture on Sarah's part has put me over the edge.

The homemade salt scrub is sweet but it's the note attached that now has me sitting amongst Pastor Seth, Sarah, mom and grandma trying desperately to hold it together. I say thank you behind eyes filling with tears as I read the words to myself: "Caring for our bodies is fine and can be fun but let's not forget that charm is deceitful and beauty is vain, but a woman that fears the Lord is to be praised." I've tried so hard to be that woman, but have mostly received the opposite of praise.

On top of that I'm still not clear on what I'm even doing here. Or what I'm expecting from Pastor Seth. Or from God for that matter. "I'm here Lord, now what?" is what I feel like shouting.

The End is Nigh

May 18

Our time here is up, for now. Between our weekend with the Jefferson's and the Extended Stay hotel this past week we have been in St. Louis for 10 days - the longest we have been in any one place. And I think we've found our home. Well, our future home. There is a church that seems rock solid, a pastor who preaches Truth unapologetically, church members who seem sweet and authentic, and an area that is both affordable right now and also has plenty of potential for business ventures.

With an extra spring in my step and an optimism that's been vacant for months, we head out on our southward drive. We can't stop the travels quite yet. We will continue on with our scheduled stays and make our way towards New York to settle a few matters, and then we'll be back! Finally, the end is nigh, thank you Lord.

Stress

May 22

The end is indeed in sight, but it's not here yet. There are still so many things to be done first. As I sit here in Alabama, in one of the more posh houses on our trip, the one concern weighing most on my mind is the question of how I am going to get back to New York City to run two training events for my job. Two non-sequential days. Where are we going to stay? Who will watch the kids? The meetings are at night, maybe I can find a hotel close to the location and slip out for the necessary two hours while the kids sleep. Insane, but what else can I do?

On top of that at some point I need to tell my boss I'm not longer local. But how can I do that until I have a location to give her. I can only imagine how the conversation might go:

"Samantha, I need to let you know that I'm no longer based out of New York. I'd like to continue with the position and can make a monthly trip into the city to do the necessary training events, but will understand if you want to find someone else."

Samantha: "Thanks for letting me know. I will get back to you with an answer. Where's home base now?"

What do I tell my boss? "We are aimlessly traveling the country?" Do I tell her 'It depends on the day, but today we are Alabamians?" How in the world can I give an honest answer without mixing business and personal? She deserves to know that New York will no longer be my home, but I have no idea how or when to tell her.

It seems the list of issues on my plate never decreases, I merely trade one set of problems for another; one concern for the next. As soon as I make one decision and put to rest one quandary another one takes its place.

Oh, how I long for a day when there are no decisions to be made and no predicaments haunting me. Oh, how I long for heaven. "Lord, help me to rest in You."

Stretched to the Max

May 24

Well that's it. We have truly run the gamut. As if I haven't been stretched enough already, God is doing it yet again. I can't help but wonder how much of this is for His own enjoyment and humor.

In college, I participated in a program called ASB - Alternate Spring Break. It served a few purposes for me, in no particular order. I was never part of the partying crowd that would head to the beach for Spring Break. That just wasn't me. I wasn't a drinker and preferred to remain fully clothed rather than prance around in a bathing suit not much different from my undergarments, looking to "hook-up" with a fellow of equally impaired morals. I also enjoyed being useful and helping others. Some of that was a sincere desire to help, some of that was faulty theology that said I could be a good person by doing good things. Regardless of all the reasons, my choices were to either hang around the mostly desolate campus over break or go do something worthwhile; so I signed up.

There were different groups going to different locations with different missions. Each trip was self-funded so while other trips may have been more appealing, cost was an overriding factor for me. So the trip traveling by bus was what fit my budget. We headed out via bus to Cleveland, OH to help with a soup kitchen at an inner city mission. A soup kitchen seemed benign enough. I could stand there and serve people food. I could still keep my distance while doing my duty. I never realized that there would be more to it than what was advertised.

We did help with the kitchen but we were also encouraged to visit the affiliated homeless shelter at some point during our week in town. *Homeless shelter, why would I want to go there? What kind of people would I meet? Will they have all their teeth? Will they stink horribly? Will I offend them because, quite honestly, I am offended by them?'*

Not only were we encouraged, but we were also reminded e v e r y s i n g l e n i g h t until one day the leaders asked in a statement kind of way, "Everyone has gone over to the shelter, right?" Everyone gave an affirmative response except me, who remained silent, hoping with all hope that I wouldn't be discovered.

I was on the trip with a desire to help, but a homeless shelter was way too far beyond my comfort zone. I mean sure, I felt bad for them. And I was glad that *someone* was willing to help them in a direct way, but it wasn't going to be me. When we all climbed back on the bus five days later I could not wait to return to my dorm room, back to the comfort and security I was used to.

So when we pull into a makeshift driveway off a rural country road, some of my prejudices once again come to light.

Jeremy Holden told me to call when we get close because the driveway is "a work in progress," and not clearly defined. Such disclaimers are nothing new at this point, but it still peaked my interest.

What could that possibly mean? We turn onto their street and drive past what I wanted to think couldn't possibly be them but also knew it was indeed their home. A mile down the road when reality hadn't changed and my dream didn't end I turned around to face the facts. They live in a trailer park.

I'm not sure why this was such a stark realization for me. I knew they lived in a trailer park from Trina's blog. Well, I knew he ran a trailer park. I suppose I had a vain hope that they lived elsewhere. But nope, double wide was our next stay.

My upbringing didn't teach me much respect for trailer folks. Nor for those under my economic level in general. For the next two days, we would be staying not only in a trailer, but in a trailer park. The Holden's might be perfectly normal, I sure hope that is the case, but who else will we encounter while staying here? I can readily recognize that my thoughts are not in keeping with Christ's attitude towards the poor and can label my prejudices as sin - but that doesn't change the fact that I have many years of indoctrination to overcome - preferably before we get to their door.

We finally find the driveway with the help of Trina, who stands at the end of the road waving us down. The Holdens do all have their teeth, with the exception of a 7-year-old who is quite excited about his missing pearly whites. And the home is, well, normal. It's a home, like any other. And it occurs to me – the stark difference between my kids and me -- not just here but with every stop. They were never impressed by the larger homes, nor put off by the smaller homes. They weren't awed by the standard of cleanliness in some families nor offended by the lack of such standard in others. People are people and homes are homes. The bigger homes did not gain more respect and admiration and the cleaner homes were not viewed and treated as superior.

Now with that background imagine my shock when mid-conversation with Trina, a shirtless man, looking as disheveled as anyone I'd ever seen, simply lets himself into the house and walks right into the kitchen. I know this isn't Jeremy. This strange and scary looking man seems quite comfortable and Trina isn't at all alarmed. In fact she hardly glances up. Clearly, he isn't seen as a danger, but who was he, why does he look the way he looks and what does he want?

Eventually he is addressed--not dressed mind you, still shirtless, but addressed. And eventually he leaves. All in all, he is here for less than 5 minutes - a very strange and uncomfortable five minutes. Amazingly, Trina isn't the least bit fazed. It's clear that Joe is a regular visitor. His sudden appearance and lack of knocking don't bother Trina one bit. Over the next two days I'd get more information about Joe.

The descriptions I hear from both Jeremy and Trina confirm my initial analysis that Joe is indeed a strange fellow, but the difference between the Holden's and myself is their acceptance of Joe and my utter discomfort with him. By now they have known Joe for over a year and both Jeremy and Trina admit that they had to warm up to Joe's uniqueness. But they had, and I'm left wondering if I am even capable of the kindness and Gospel grace I see emanating from Trina and Jeremy and the extended Holden clan. It is both encouraging and humbling all at once.

The Holden's are a blue collar folk. Your everyday average family - normal background, decent paycheck, good education. So for them to invest in a trailer park and *move in* was as much of a culture shock for them as it is for me - yet they are navigating the change while maintaining such a Christian testimony.

*****

The Holdens made us feel welcome from the moment we arrived. Their kids are eager for some new playmates - the ages of whom line up quite nicely with my own kiddos. Conversation with Jeremy and Trina seems painless and natural and the more we talk the more we realize all we have in common. Likeminded in so many ways. So it is no surprise to me now that as we chatted and as Trina asked questions about our travels more of my story came out than I normally share. It is this very lady you can thank (or curse - depending on your opinion thus far) for having this story in your hands.

As I recount our departure from New York to start the trip, it's as if she is connecting the dots in her mind until she suddenly blurts out, "wait a minute, are you saying that you are on this trip right now because you don't have anywhere else to be?" There is no wiggle room in answering that question and so I concede the corner I'm in and answer affirmatively. With that she replies, "Wow, you need to write your story." And thus you now have in your hands, <u>Journey to Somewhere</u>.

*****

Our time with the Holdens goes fast. It's two days of wonderful conversation for me and playtime for my kids. As we are preparing to leave Trina says, "If you decide you need to park it somewhere for a while you are welcome back here. We have the converted bus that we used when we first moved down here. You are more than welcome to stay in there for a while."

While Alabama was never on my list of possible locations and I hope I won't need to accept her offer, it is a tremendous relief to know that the travels can now end at any time. But at the moment it's nothing more than a nice sentiment because we are still heading back to St. Louis.

Faithful Friends

May 30

Word comes back from Samantha that they are going to look for a new person to fill my role. I will finish out June, but this was meant to be a local position. I don't fault her for a moment nor do I question the Lord. He has been faithful thus far and will continue to be so. He is the one, after all, who provided this job at the exact moment I needed it and He will surely provide another one in due time. So I feel a peace about it, to a degree - so long as my eyes are fixed on Him and not on the storm around me.

But without the job St. Louis just isn't an option. I no longer have the means for an apartment and cannot take that big of a leap and risk with only a hope that something will come through. So once again I am back at square one with the same old question, "What next Lord? Where to?"

I have purposed to enjoy our travels as much as possible, but I am ready to be done and to settle. What will that look like? And will it even ever happen? I do know that this is exactly where God wants me because it is exactly where I am. He is teaching me to trust Him completely; to lean not on my own understanding. My understanding is lacking. I can't make heads or tails of any of it, but He will guide my steps and I need to keep my eyes fixed on Him and Him alone.

That may sound super spiritual and I'd like to say that I've come to this conclusion all on my own, but the truth is I am much indebted to a faithful friend who has been a constant source of encouragement, reminding me to turn to Christ with each and every hurdle. We spoke yet again today. As I once again share my fear and frustration amidst such certainty, Allison once again reminds me of the many evidences of God's faithfulness thus far and encourages me to press on in obedience to Him. He will make it clear when the time comes.

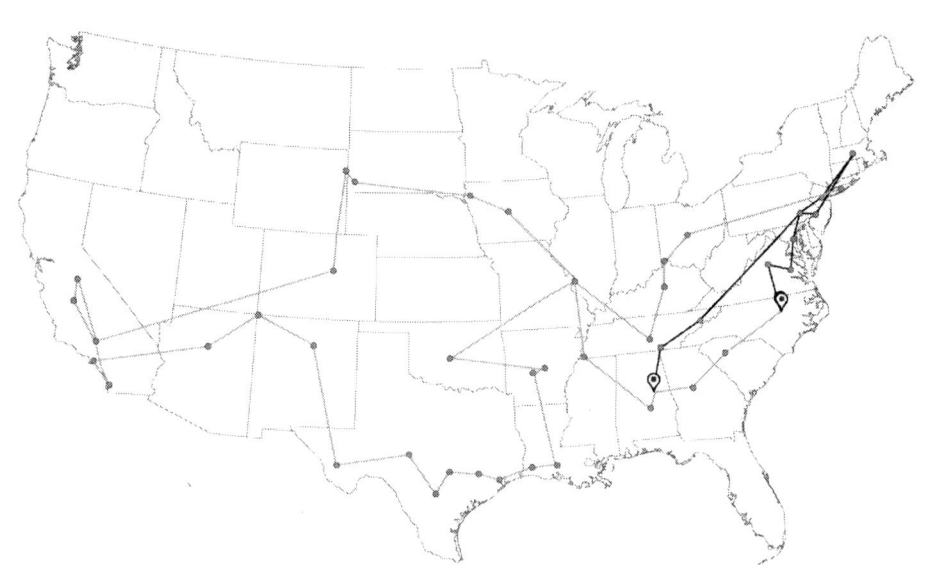

Part Three

Delighting in the Lord

Undecided

June 2

There is no hurry this morning. We don't have much of a destination. With a last minute change of plans there is really nothing on the agenda other than to cover some miles in a northwardly direction. Sickness popped up in the Michael's house, which was supposed to be our next stop, so we have two days to figure out, two days of lodging to arrange.

Maybe we will head to Williamsburg, Virginia; I've always wanted to go there. But at the same time, with the impending end of my job, I am holding on to every dollar I possibly can. I suspect Williamsburg is wonderful, so long as one is willing to spend a decent amount of money. Right now, I'm aiming at spending as little as possible.

We all get up and get dressed. I set the girls up in the kitchen with breakfast duty. They love the responsibility and quite honestly I need to be less lazy in the area of teaching and training them to cook. They help me make the pancake batter and then I leave them to cook the pancakes while I start to pack up. I don't get very far into the packing before there is a child wanting my attention. Instead of packing I sit down with Austin and coo at baby Calvin. Oh, he is just too cute!

The kids start eating on the fly, too impatient to wait for the whole batch to be cooked. So pancake by pancake the spoils are divided up and my children chow down. The thrill of cooking ends shortly after and Abigail asks if "I would like to cook the rest." "Sure, my darling, I'd be happy to finish up."

They now transition to the table with requests for syrup pouring in. While I cook, I enjoy some last minute chat time with Cassandra. It has been so good to spend time with her and her budding family. Crazy to think we've been friends for 15 years - almost half of our lives. We have had some rocky moments in our friendship but hers is the longest meaningful friendship I've ever had. There are plenty of people I have known longer, but at this point they are more acquaintances than true, solid friends.

She and I have been friends since the very first day of college. We have stood by each other through school challenges, job frustrations, weddings and babies. She has seen me at my worst, including in my days before conversion. It would be interesting to ask her what she sees in me today versus what she saw in me during our years at Penn....but I don't have the guts to ask.

The kids finish eating and it's really time to finish packing. I know we don't have a destination, but we do need to make some progress towards our next stop. Cassandra entertains the girls with more crochet talk while I pack up and load the car.

I return to the house to find Cassandra re-rolling a ball of yarn that Annabella managed to dishevel between last night and now. It's a task I think I would avoid at all costs, but Cassandra seems to be genuinely enjoying the process. I am so grateful for friends that are crafty because I am not!

The boredom is too much for my two tiger cubs and wrestling ensues in and around the living room. Poor Mark, Cassandra's husband, is trying to work in his upstairs office but I'm sure it's a futile attempt with the level of noise down here. Mindful of the volume, I send Alexander outside and immediately the decibel level dramatically decreases.

Within minutes Mark is downstairs, probably eager to know the cause of the drastic volume change. Cassandra informs him that Alexander is outside and without a word Mark makes an abrupt exit. I scan the yard from their large bay window to make sure I can still see Alexander. Not that I'm concerned about him leaving the property. We are sitting on seven acres and are a mile back from the road – I have no concern that Alexander is going to walk off. But it's still wise to get a visual every so often.

I look out and see Alexander squatting down, seemingly inspecting a crawling creature of some sort and Mark right there next to him, also squatting and pointing as he talks to Alexander. My heart leaps with joy. Stupid, right? But for my son, this is HUGE.

Alexander is getting some man-time, which he so desperately needs. Not only is he getting attention and interaction from an adult other than mom (whom he sees 24/7), but it's from a man. There is something about little boys needing male influence, and I just can't offer that.

Mark had been so good to him; to all of my kids, but especially the boys. He is so patient and finds opportunities to teach them in the midst of everyday activities. It's a wonderful trait to have and it excites me to know that Calvin has this kind of a dad.

Mark comes back inside and Cassandra is still winding yarn. He stands resolute and boldly declares that he and Alexander had a solid conversation about bees. Mark and Cassandra have a number of underground bee hives along their driveway, sand bees is what they call them. I have no idea the content of the conversation beyond bees, but I know that brief interaction will carry my son for a while.

Cassandra finally finishes the yarn and we say our goodbyes. Calvin, of course, receives the bulk of attention from my kids as we go. I know we will see them again, just another road trip away.

*****

Last Minute Plans

Thirty minutes into our drive towards Williamsburg, Abigail asks if we can go hiking again. "We sure can, but the mountains should be where we head if you want to hike, not the coast." So we make a u-turn and retrace our steps back almost to where we started in order to make the necessary adjustments to head towards western Virginia.

I'm not too thrilled with the prospect of two days in a hotel, specifically the cost of two days in a hotel. It is totally last minute and a long shot, but I take the chance and email another network family. "At least if we do end up in a hotel I know I did everything I could to avoid it," I console myself.

It doesn't take long before an email reply is sitting in my inbox saying they "can make it work." "Make it work," I love that mindset. It isn't planned, it isn't scheduled, but somehow they will rearrange their life to some degree to "make it work."

I call right away as requested to work out the details. Their usual guest apartment is occupied at the moment but they can swing it with an air mattress, sleeping bags and shifting kids. What amazing hospitality. Willing to be totally inconvenienced and welcome in 5 strangers with only a one-day notice. Tonight we will stay in a hotel, but tomorrow is covered.

By now it is well past lunch time and the kids are hungry. On long driving days, I can go much longer than them between meals. I'd likely be fine up until dinner, but four little bellies say otherwise. We make a quick pit stop for potty breaks and then head straight across the street. On our way into the gas station, I saw a sign for a park, a perfect place to have a picnic and stretch our legs. As we shoot straight across the highway, a pickup turns in behind us.

I will confess I drive rather fast sometimes. I'd like to use the excuse that I inherited a lead foot from my mother, a nickname given to her by my father, but such things are not actually genetic so the truth is that I dislike going slow. In and around my hometown I know the limits that will likely lead to a ticket, but as we travel from state to state I rely on the locals to gauge my speed. So as we follow the signs leading to the park, I keep a steady distance in front of the truck. As long as he isn't on my rear bumper I know I'm not going too slow and as long as I can see him in my mirror I'm not going too fast. But I soon grow impatient with the slow pace of the truck and with my genetic lead food itching to go faster the truck is soon out of view.

I manage to drive right past the park entrance – surely it has nothing to do with my speed – and catch the mistake just as my head turns to read, "Park Entrance →" As I slow down looking for a place to turn around the truck is now once again in view. I pull down the next street to let the truck pass and to turn around; the truck turns too. "That's weird," I think to myself.

We drive down a little ways until I finally see a patch of grass wide enough to enable a u-turn, but as I pull over the pickup slows down and stops right next to us. "Um, what is he doing?" I think slightly nervously.

He looks at me through his fully closed passenger window as I look back at him through my slightly cracked window with much skepticism. I try to wave him on, he doesn't move. He is saying something through his window but I have no idea what. Finally, he gestures in such a way that lessens my suspicion and as he leans over to roll down his window I open mine a wee bit more.

"Just want to make sure you are okay," he says, cigar in his mouth. "We are fine, just turning around," I reply. "Alright" he says with a thick southern drawl, "where are y'all headed down here. Are you lost?" "No, we aren't lost. We are headed to the park back there." "Alright. Just making sure you're alright." And with that he drives on.

We turn around and head straight into the park. It's a strange park; rather secluded with a peculiar layout. To the left of the narrow dirt entryway we pass ball fields that sit behind a sparsely treed gully. We turn a corner and now to the right sits a playground and picnic area. To the left is an open field. Aside from the three vehicles at the far end of the park sitting adjacent a backhoe the park is empty.

Interesting.

I pull into a parking spot. Well, actually I don't know if it's a parking spot. It's a curved area on the road, but with so few people, I don't think it matters much where we park. We all climb out of the car, the kids are as eager to play as they are to eat. As they run off to the playground, I step around to the back of the car to gather our food.

Silence. Utter, eerie silence. I hear my kids playing and the gentle breeze blowing the leaves on the trees but beyond that is an uncomfortable quiet. Self-defense brain kicks in yet again (apparently my 16 years of martial arts training have not all been forgotten): "This is rather remote. We are without any fellas. If we had to make a quick departure for some reason we would not be able to - the road in was windy, narrow and with heavy woods on either side. I've seen enough horror films in my pagan years to know that this was the making of such a story."

"Kids, we are going to eat and then get right back in the car. I'm not comfortable staying here any longer than necessary. You can play while I prep the food but then you need to eat." Groans and moans ensue and my girls ask why I'm uncomfortable.

How in the world do I explain to them, "Well honey, I just don't want to make the 6 o'clock news as the family who was chopped up and strewn about the park" without causing fright?

"Wisdom, sweetheart. God wants us to use wisdom and it just isn't wise to be at a park like this without any other adults here with us." "But we go to other parks by ourselves," comes the objection. "Yes, honey, but those parks usually have other people. And they aren't hidden away like this one. Even if no one else is at those other parks, they are near a road so there are constantly people driving by."

That explanation will have to do because saying any more would not be beneficial to their innocent little minds. They know there are bad people in the world. They know some people seek out opportunity to hurt others. They've read about violence in the Bible and we have talked about being cautious towards potential dangers. But they do not need to know the scenario that is playing out in my mind.

At Ease

June 3

We take our time driving today. A direct route would take less than two hours but we have a whole day to kill. My excitement about our travels comes in cycles. Today, it's on a down cycle - I merely want to get through the day. The stress of it all can feel unbearable at times. The constant need to arrange new stays, to plan new routes, to buy time for...for what? I don't even know. I no longer have an end game. I thought it was all settled, I hoped it was all settled, but with St. Louis no longer the destination I once again have no plan.

After a meandering day of driving and visiting various parks along the way, we arrive at the Cringle home. We are greeted on the front porch by an older woman who perplexes me. "We are looking for Ed and Monica Cringle, are we at the right house?" She assures me we are and I presume her to be either Monica or Ed's mom. She leads us through the front door. There is a staircase to the left as soon as we enter, a large sitting room to the right, an open loft area as I look up and straight ahead a large open kitchen from where I hear a cheerful, "Hello, welcome." Monica Cringle is prepping dinner and quickly comes over carrying with her a huge, warm smile. "Welcome," she says again.

Her friendly and relaxed demeanor puts me right at ease. After the requisite greetings, my girls made a b-line back out the front door to the huge tree swing they spotted when we pulled up. The boys have just woken up from naps and are slower to acclimate. I hold Austin (3) in my arms as Alexander (5) attempts to hide behind my leg, leaving me slightly embarrassed that he won't say hello. And I do mean slightly. A month ago, I would have been horribly embarrassed, but along this trip I have grown more and more confident in my own skin and less apologetic about my kids being kids.

Monica doesn't seem at all bothered by what might have been construed as rudeness. "It's tough for them," she says with all sincerity, "constantly meeting new people and waking up in new places." I had never thought of it like that, but she is right. Her easy going nature is truly refreshing and continues throughout our short one night stay.

Later on as dinner cooks in the oven, Monica joins me in the living room where I am sitting with my boys. Noticing that they don't seem comfortable enough to leave my side yet, but also antsy needing something to do she calls one of her children to bring down a basket of Duplo blocks. As we chat intermittently, Monica seems sincerely content to watch them play and encourages them in their building.

Along this journey, I have slowly become aware of the theological error that pervaded my thoughts at the onset of the trip. Firstly, a fear of man: a sinful concern about what others think of me and whether I meet up to their expectations; as though I can read minds and know the various expectations from house to house.

Secondly, if someone takes offense at me, not because I'm sinning against them and not because I'm being a rude and inconsiderate guest, but for some other reason, then it is not my problem, but theirs. And more accurately, not my sin, but theirs. If they are placing judgment on me for something the Lord does not judge me for then they are in sin, plain and simple. So why have I spent so much time fearing the opinions of others when I am already loved by the only One whose opinion ultimately matters?

I am in the Beloved. I am accepted by the Creator, who bled and died to forgive my sins. That same Creator disciplines those whom He loves and if I am being a rude guest in some way then I am no longer properly representing Him, because He is not rude, and some correction may be in order. But short of that, the opinion of my host towards my family and me is irrelevant.

On the flip side, to have such fear is an insult to my host. It contains an assumption that my host is not a gracious host. These are Christian families that claim to love and serve the same Jesus Christ that I love and serve. They are sinful people on the long journey of sanctification, just as I am. If I don't enter a home with a mind to judge their outfits, their children, the quality of their food, etc.. then why would I expect them to do that towards me, especially after they have graciously invited us in? How bizarre it would be for a Christian family to voluntarily take part in a hospitality network so that they can have some kind of twisted "fun" by judging their guests.

Additionally, such fears leave out the possibility that my host might actually have the same insecurities as a host that I do as a guest. Maybe joining this network and hosting strangers is a tremendous stretch and growth area for them. One family admitted as such by our second day. As I enter a home worried about what they think, my host might be equally concerned about what I think. I can imagine some of those fears because I've had many in the few occasions I've hosted: is the house clean enough? Are my kids going to behave? What if they don't like the type of food we eat? What if they find me boring?

It is a joy and a relief when the demeanor of a host is relaxed and puts me at ease. But maybe I should be less concerned about what to expect and instead focus on my own demeanor and how I might put a nervous host at ease. Even in my worries I'm selfish. All my thoughts are of self; self preservation, putting forth a good image, even a false image because the truth is my kids DO sometimes misbehave, yet I want them to be perfect little angels everywhere we go. And, of course, I'm on my best behavior when we enter a home as well. I'll save my impatience for the car rides when no one else (aside from my kids and Jesus) can see. Not quite authentic.

Grand Estates and Humble Beginnings

June 4

Our drive today is a short one -- same city, opposite side. I'm excited because this means we can have a full day of sightseeing with minimal car time. We were told by the Cringle's, "You can't come to Charlottesville and not visit Monticello." And so, Monticello, which we will later learn means "Little Mountain" in Italian, is the agenda for today.

Ah, the famous Monticello, Thomas Jefferson's masterpiece, his home on that Virginia hillside. I've never been here before but like most Americans I am very familiar with the dome. It feels a bit surreal as we pull into the parking lot. I am going to Thomas Jefferson's home. Thomas Jefferson - that famous statesman. Thomas Jefferson - the one who penned the Declaration of Independence. Thomas Jefferson - the masterful inventor. And that's about all I know, but I'm feeling nostalgic nonetheless.

We purchase our tour tickets and make our way to the bus that will transport us the one-mile drive up to the house. We still have almost an hour until our tour time, but I have no desire to cut it close. One can never tell how long it will take to gather four children - what sort of emergency potty breaks will be necessary, or other child issues. So we'll eat our lunch picnic-style somewhere on the lawn while we wait for our tour time.

As we take the winding road up, and I do mean up -- remember, "little mountain" -- I picture Thomas (we're on a first name basis now) returning home after a long excursion away, "official business" of course. He's on horseback. His family waits eagerly for any sight of father as his horse gallantly strides up the incline, white powdered wig blowing in the wind. It could have happened, right?

I'm snapped out of my dreamlike state as we come to a stop just outside the lawn area. We hop off the bus and find a cozy spot on the right lawn to sit and eat. "Right lawn" - I love how fancy houses have "lawns" designated by direction. The house I once owned had a front yard and a back yard, and with that I was feeling pretty special. But my house paled in comparison to the grand Monticello.

You'd need a bit more specificity when making plans to meet someone here. You couldn't just say, "I'll meet you out front". There could potentially be an acre or two between you and them. Instead, "I'll meet you on the south front lawn" greatly increases the likelihood of finding one another.

Anyway, we sit in the shade provided by one of the many trees on the property. While we eat we enjoy the view of tour guides dressed in period pieces taking groups of tourists up the front steps and into the house. *This is so cool*, I think to myself – though dare not say out loud lest I be *uncool*. I wonder if Tom and his family ever sat out here to picnic. Did he ever walk where we are now seated? How many delegates passed this way? I'm enjoying my moments of wonder when I see our tour group heading towards the house. '"Quickly kids, there goes our group" I say as I pack up our lunch fix-ins as fast as possible and zip closed the cooler bag. We run, every man for himself, and fall into line just as our group reaches the steps that lead to the front door.

Our tour guide is an enthusiastic fellow. Not young but not old either. He speaks quickly, but is easy to understand. He clearly enjoys his job, or else is a fantastic actor. He recites the tour speech for us as if it's the first time today rather than the fifth or sixth, which is more likely. As soon as we walk through the door the fear of disappointed expectations is relieved. I am looking at Jefferson's house with Jefferson's things. On the wall around the front door is his calendar system. He rigged the clock that sits above the door to also keep track of days of the week in an elaborate system that I won't pretend to understand.

We make our way room by room learning history along the way. What was the purpose of this room? Who used this room? There is a *special* guest room. It's the VIP room where Tom's favorite visitors would stay. What makes this room special you ask? From what I can gather it's the extra walls -- four to be specific. It is an octagonal room with the bed set into the wall. I'm not sure what is more impressive - the alcove bed, or the eight walls or the amount of floor space resulting from the alcove bed. If I had to pick it would be the amount of floor space only because we have seen an alcove bed before. (Passing through Orange City, IA we toured a Dutch windmill house with an alcove bed – one of the numerous fascinating aspects of architecture we saw there). The VIP visitors that most often stayed here were none other than James and Dolly Madison.

But my favorite room is Jefferson's own bedroom.

His is a larger room with a partial wall in the center that both housed his alcove bed and provided a division in the room. One side of the room is set up for bedroom functions and he likely entered his bed at night from this side. In the morning, he could roll out the other side of the bed and be immediately in his work area. Or, I suppose, he could walk through the doorway as we did, but that's not nearly as fun. It all brings new meaning to saying, "woke up on the wrong side of the bed."

I am dazzled throughout the tour by this magnificent home. I picture his wife and children enjoying all the many luxuries here. There are rooms to host guests. A huge *lawn* to enjoy. Beautiful gardens to enjoy both for beauty and for the various produce. "How easy it would be to show hospitality with a home like this," I muse to myself. "If nothing else, my own pride would prompt me to invite people over so they could see my beautiful home, I mean enjoy fellowship." If I lived in Monticello surely I'd schedule regular times to host people.

But looks can be deceiving.

Even Monticello is not without its quirks. Jefferson was ahead of his time with the technology that filled each and every room. Not as an inventor as I thought at the onset of the tour, but rather as a tinkerer, improving upon inventions. He took the tools of the day and improved them. But there were still forces he couldn't change, like the harsh Virginia winters. Double paned glass doors would close off a entire dining area in winter because of the cold, rendering the room unusable until spring.

So much for perfection.

And while Jefferson began building in 1769, it was not completed until 1809. Oh sure, Jefferson was promoting world peace in France for a time and writing the Declaration in there as well. He was a busy man. But 40 years of construction in one form or another. Far from the pristine picture I had in my mind of the near-perfect home for wife and children.

Additionally, I have always assumed that Jefferson was a wealthy man. He was a statesman. He owned land, slaves, and was well traveled. He was well-read, with one of the most extensive book collections of his time. But the reality is that he died while in significant debt.

My awe and wonder for the home I see before me is not diminished by this newfound knowledge, but the fanciful make-believe world I created in my mind has been shattered. Despite the highlights we like to remember about people, there is a reality of life – put simply, life is hard. Nothing is perfect. No situation is perfect. No man or woman is perfect. Hardships and trials come. But in the midst of life we can either persevere, creating our own "Monticello" with **40 years** of labor or shrivel and shrink back thus missing all that *could be.*

I started the day with Monticello being a surreal dream and finished realizing that Jefferson faced the same life challenges as the rest of us. But in the midst of constant construction, a very hectic personal and professional life, less than hospitable weather and even extreme debt, Jefferson remained hospitable. He loved entertaining. He loved conversing over dinner. He enjoyed people and enjoyed their company. I could say he did all of these things despite circumstances, but maybe it was because of them.

Our trip has allowed us to see a wide spectrum of homes. And the "WOW" homes that cause me to think, "I would love this house" come with the false assumption that what I see is what *always* was. I arrived at Monticello not at all wondering the process it took to create Monticello. Simply, "this is his home" as if this was always his home just as it looks today. This false notion has come to light at various stops along the way.

The West Texas family lived in a trailer for **seven years** on their dream property while they patiently saved to build their dream home. A southern family relocated a few years ago so that their eldest son could pursue his dream of farming. They bought land then designed and built their dream home. Their family life didn't start out this way. That wasn't the house Mr. & Mrs. moved into after the honeymoon. It came after 20+ years of marriage. Or the grand home in the mountains that I assumed was owned by what must be a very successful professional of sorts was actually a rental.

But whether the home was owned or rented, huge or tiny, whether the family was in the 1% or deeply in debt, a consistent vein ran through each and every house on our stay – a heart for hospitality. Each house along the way has invited us in, provided a place to sleep and a meal to eat. Each one has been pleased to have us, eager to hear about our travels and learn about us. It's the mindset that matters, not the externals. I suspect TJ would still have regularly hosted dinner parties even if he lived in a one room cabin because hospitality was part of his character, not just something he did.

Our Nation's Capitol

June 7

Today is supposed to be an enjoyable day of tourism in our nation's capital. Instead, thus far, it's been a morning of mom being irritable at life. I can't seem to escape the stresses of life and, it seems, I am failing to truly trust the Lord. "Be anxious for nothing, but in everything by prayer and supplication make your request known to

Annabella excited for DC.

God and the peace of God which surpasses all understanding will guard your heart and mind in Christ Jesus." "Trust in the Lord with all your heart and lean not on your own understanding. In all your ways acknowledge Him and He will make straight your paths." And could Jesus be any clearer in Matthew 6:25-34 where He starts with "Therefore I tell you, do not be anxious about your life, what you will eat or what you will drink, nor about your body, what you will put on. Is not life more than food and the body more than clothing?" and ends with "Therefore do not be anxious about tomorrow, for tomorrow will be anxious for itself. Sufficient for the day is its own trouble."

Here I am, very anxious about my life and about what we will eat and drink, where we will live; the mundane aspects of life. I am very anxious about tomorrow. When will I learn to wake in the morning and pray, "Lord, give me *today* what I need. Provide for us this day. Enable me to accomplish *today* what you have for me and to not fret about tomorrow?" That needs to be my daily mindset and daily prayer.

DC Metro

Your Reputation Precedes You

June 9

This is by far the most anticipated stay of our whole trip. We have come almost full circle and are near our starting point, although we won't be traveling anywhere near "home." One of the first families I contacted as we departed three months ago was the Burns family. It seemed every few weeks we'd stay with a network family that knew the Burns' and had nothing but wonderful things to say. My intrigue for this woman, who went above and beyond to help us find a place to stay early on, was growing and she was becoming a bit of a legend.

I write these words at their nearest Starbucks. We will be leaving the Burns' home in just a few hours, but for now I am sitting with my six year old beside me, enjoying the quiet of a coffee shop with some time to read, reflect and write while the Burns' clan is looking after my other three children.

It is rare for me to leave my children with anyone. I am so wary of the evil in this world, even amongst folks that seem trustworthy. There are too many teenage boys in the news for abusing little kids they know. No matter how trustworthy a family or a person seems on the outside, it takes much more than superficial appearances to earn my trust, especially when it comes to my children. So it is a rare thing indeed that I have left three of my children in their care for a few hours this morning.

As I reflect over the last few days, our time with the Burns family is surely one of the highlights of our trip. Jamie and crew have exceeded the reputation set for them by so many of the families along the way. They have truly been a joy to meet and an encouragement to talk with. And most of all, they have given me something to consider.

Up until two years ago, the Burns' were in San Antonio - and had been there for over a decade. They loved that area and are hopeful to one day return. As they spoke with fondness about the people, the friends they left behind (including the Petroski's), about the Christian culture and the niche of homeschoolers they found there, San Antonio has grown more and more attractive. Maybe St. Louis was to give me hope at a time when I desperately needed it, but maybe the inclination I had about San Antonio back in April was right on. "Lord, is that what you have for us?"

A ray of hope once again appears.

We are soon on our way waving goodbye and promising to stop back in when we pass back through their area. Right now the plan is to buy time. To make as many network stops as I can, just get from day to day while I continue to wait on the Lord for direction and guidance. So we leave the Burns' and head over the state line into New Jersey for no other purpose than to get two days into the future.

Our time with the Burns family was nothing short of refreshing, but the travels continue on with no end in sight and I am rather worn out – worn out from the constant logistical juggling, worn out from life as a tourist, worn out from the emotional drain of the circumstances. And now with my job ending in less than thirty days I'm not very gung-ho about touristy activities. I'm just ready to be done. The goal for each day is to get to bedtime as fast as possible, which just

A family portrait taken by the very talented Julie Smithe

takes me closer to…something else. That much closer to some unknown future. Each day is merely an act of procrastination as I wait for what the Lord has planned next.

It makes me think of my time in Europe between freshman and sophomore year in college. Freshman year ended rather rough. I was recruited to play soccer and did so in the fall my first year. A few weeks after the season ended I let the coach know I would not be returning to the team. Soccer had lost all of its fun and I simply did not want to play any longer.

The conversation with the coach made my departure official and I was completely blindsided by the overwhelming emotions that followed. All my life I defined myself as a soccer player. It was more than what I did -- it was who I was. Now I was no longer defined in that way and I had no idea who I was or what my purpose would be. I came back from winter break ten pounds heavier. How a collegiate athlete gains ten pounds over a three week break is still a mystery to me, but my coping mechanism was food. I will forever be reminded of that time and the weight gain when I look at my passport photo, taken in the spring semester in preparation for my trip to Europe.

I had a desire to travel and in hindsight I think it was recognition that I was missing something, or more accurately Someone. I did not know it at the time, but the desire to travel, to explore, to keep moving was all about finding truth. Truth would find me in His good time a few years later and would use this period of struggle to do so. But Europe was calling my name and a week after the school year ended I was on a plane to England.

The plan was to work for two months through a program called BUNAC, which allowed non-nationals to work temporarily. After working and saving up a bunch of money I'd then travel for the remaining month of the summer throughout Europe.

Less than a week into the job, I had enough. There was nothing wrong with the job itself; it actually seemed interesting. And there was certainly nothing wrong with the location. I was at the famous Cambridge University. It was me. I was uncomfortable. It was way too far outside of my comfort zone and I wanted no part of it.

I notified my boss that I was done as well as the lady from whom I rented a room. I lost $750 in rent because of the short notice, but I didn't care. I knew I couldn't stay there and I couldn't do the job I was hired to do. I walked away from a tremendous opportunity out of fear and I decided to travel.

I promptly hopped a ferry over to France and began my journey. Totally winging it, I made my way into Paris and looked for a hostel. *(In the days before the internet was ubiquitous and the standard method of booking a hostel was on a website, my options were either using a payphone or walking into the location to book in person.)*

Well, it must have been a busy time because every hostel in Paris was full. So I did what any logical 19 year old would do; I went to the train station, looked at the board and said "that looks like an interesting city" and off I was to Tours.

I was in Tours for three days - not soaking up the culture, not trying to learn some French nor exploring the city. Nope. I woke up each morning with only one thought on my mind – how long until bed-time?

The depression I thought I had escaped during second semester returned and I wanted nothing more than to sleep through my days. It was an endless cycle of waking and then wishing it was night already just so the next day could arrive and I could once again long for bedtime.

It has been years since I've been plagued by that level of depression, but the desire to pass the days quickly has returned. Daytime seems pointless as we have no plan, and I see no light to indicate the end of the tunnel. Any future plan I might develop is pointless since I cannot see past today and therefore can see no means of achieving any goal and dream. Right now a place to sleep and food to eat is about all I aspire to and the faster the days go the sooner the end will come.

So our New Jersey stop is simply a place to hang for two days - somewhere to sleep for two days - to get us two days closer to whatever is next.

Just Do Something

June 11

San Antonio sounds good and well, but how in the world will I make that work? I am stressed to the max about my current job, which will be ending soon anyway. I know I can generate income, I'm certain of it. It won't look like a typical 9-5 but enough small streams of income will be enough to support us. But it still feels like a thousand miles between here and there. Well, technically there are 1,694 miles between here and there, but it feels like there is an unconquerable chasm separating nomad-Melissa from settled-Melissa.

I still need money to get settled. A deposit on a place to rent. But who will rent to someone without a steady paycheck? And on top of that renting limits some of my income options. Certain opportunities will require a place without a landlord who will dictate what I can and cannot do while renting – in other words, pet sitting is out. To pursue a work at home opportunity I need a separate room to serve as my office with a landline phone. But the rent I can afford is not anywhere near what I would need for that many bedrooms.

Using my background and even the skills I've gained at this current position, I can open a niche consulting business, but it takes time to develop a client base and I need to know there are people I trust and are willing to help by watching my kids from time to time.

So in theory San Antonio is great, but there are still so many practical considerations that need to be worked out.

In the midst of that stress, I cannot find a single other home for a network stay. I know it's rather last minute, so that doesn't work in my favor. I procrastinated too much while at the Burns'. I got a bit too comfortable and deluded myself, forgetting about the reality in front of me. I kept hoping it would just all go away, and of course it didn't. So now I'm stuck.

We are heading to Massachusetts today to visit Old Sturbridge Village – quite honestly more for me than for the kids. I want to visit there. I want a glimpse at life in the early 1800's. But from there I have no idea what's next. Every attempt at lining up a stay has not worked out so there is no point in going any further north than that.

With the four hour drive before us I take the suggestion of a friend and listen to John MacArthur's sermon, "Knowing God's Will." Allison has checked in with me every step of the way on our journey and has been an incredible source of encouragement. She has been a faithful friend who has helped me keep my wits about me, pointing me back to God's faithfulness and reminding me of the care and provision He has already shown. She knows the decisions I face and if she says this is a sermon I need to hear, I heed her advice.

So as we drive today I have an ear bud in my left ear and the sermon playing on my phone. Forty four minutes later, after breaking down the Scripture and explaining what it means, Dr. MacArthur concludes with this thought: "Delight yourself in the Lord and do whatever you want."

It's not about a magic formula, it's not about reading signs in the sky, it's not about finding the *only* right decision and if I miss it then God's plan is ruined. No! Be a Spirit-filled, Bible reading believer, seek wisdom from the Word and from wise counsel. With a heart submitted to God I am then free to choose whatever is most appealing to me. And because I am Spirit filled and submitted I won't be choosing sin. And God tells us in Psalm 37:4 that when we delight ourselves in Him, He will then put His desire into our hearts, so we can choose freely without fear. What freedom!

"Delight yourself in the Lord and do whatever you want." That seems to make it all clear. No more fretting. No more fear. Still don't know all that the Lord will do – the future remains unknown, but my next step is now clear. "Lord, we are heading south!"

June 12

The course is set! To Alabama we head. With the email reply from Trina saying yes, her offer still stands about the bus, we are about to turn our ship southward. We have an opportunity to park it for a while. Time to rest. Time to think. Time to be still and regroup. For right now, this is exactly what we need to do. The future will come soon enough and new decisions will surely need to be made but for the near future we will have a place to stay. This is a short-term plan for a long-term problem, but a necessary step. And for the first time in over three months, I have complete peace.

Epilogue
Sweet Rest

We arrived in Alabama on June 16, 2014. 102 days after we departed from New York. One popped tire. Two oil changes. 34 different families. 34 different states. 10,974 miles. It's been a long journey in many respects. It took five weeks to fully unload everything from the car. It was a slow process, partly because the bus had limited storage space, but also because I knew that this too was a temporary stay.

Our "home" for 3 1/2 months.

A 15 week stay to be exact. On September 29 we moved into our very own apartment. I knew the bus was temporary, but assumed so was Alabama. Unexpectedly, what I found was a vibrant church body that welcomed us with nothing but love and kindness, and as the days and weeks went on I realized that there was no reason to leave the area. The friends we made in the last few months were exactly the kind of people I wanted to be around.

With the immense generosity of folks from our new church home, a few IKEA trips later and our apartment transformed from a place with blow up mattresses and no furniture to a home of rest and tranquility.

Rest. Sweet rest. I haven't felt rest like this in many years. There is a calmness to our lives that is indescribable. I still don't have answers for everything. This still isn't the life I had planned for myself, but apparently it is exactly what God had planned. Here we are.

I still have a vision for a house. Rooms we can paint. A backyard to run around and play in. Land to grow a garden. Space to show hospitality to others. Who knows, maybe in my future I will host a mom with children, traveling because they have nowhere else to go and my warm hospitality will be honey to her soul and refreshment for her spirit. Maybe my example will be what gives her strength to keep trusting God despite outward circumstances.

Work of some sort is likely in my future but how that will look I do not know.

I don't know what the Lord has for our future but that doesn't stop me from petitioning Him with my dreams. The reality of life as a single mom is daunting. I am a mom first. Every decision I make for us starts with "How will this impact my primary role as their mother and their teacher?" I've been told more than once to put them into public school and *just go get a job*. Aside from my opinions on the best methods to educate my children, following this advice would merely trade one set of problems for another. It is easy enough to throw out this *solution* when you aren't the one carrying it out.

On my end this is how the *easy solution* plays out:

If I put them into school that still leaves the youngest who is only three. So on this course of action he would go into a daycare for 8 or more hours per day. How much of my income will be eaten by day care costs? Then there is the logistics of three school schedules, one day care schedule and one work schedule.

Either someone gets my kids on the bus in the morning (that costs money) or is here to take them off the bus in the afternoon (also costs money) or both. What happens if one of my kids is sick and cannot go to school? Do I miss work to be with them (loss of wages) or do I hire a babysitter (money). And once the kids are in school and daycare the likelihood of getting sick grows tremendously. so really it isn't a question of "what if" but of "when" and "how often."

What do I do over school vacations and in the summer when I have to work and they are off?

Even if I could make enough money to offset the extra expenses of babysitting, a new wardrobe for work, extra gas, etc, would we be any better off than we are now? Would life really be any better off financially? Or would I simply be following a cultural trend while trading in my children for career advancement and prestige?

There is also a false assumption that I can walk back into the work-force right where I left off. That the salary I made when I put in my notice is the salary I'll make if I secure a job tomorrow. That is not likely to happen. So what income will I really take home?

I stated before that I rarely leave my kids with other people. There are many reasons for that – for one, I like my kids. I enjoy being with them. But also, no one can love them like I can as their mother. In God's design for life parents love their children and are the right and best ones to care for those children. Then add to that the concern for safety which, to ignore in today's world is simply foolish.

So with all of that, you can be sure that before I make a decision that will require me to leave my children five days a week for 8-10 hours a day I must be very, very sure it is the best decision. Not easiest or most convenient or most popular, but **best**.

My educational background has increased the pressure I have received from others to return to work. I have a degree from an Ivy League school that happens to also be one of the top business schools in the country. There is a belief by some that I have "thrown away" my degree - truthfully those people thought that the moment my husband and I stated I would be quitting work to be at home with our first child.

By walking away from corporate America 8 years ago, I traded in $689,961 for the joy and privilege of being home with my children. And that amount is without bonuses or promotions. Over the last 8 years had I continued to work at the same salary I left I would be $689,961 richer. But I'd be poorer.

I'd be poorer, because I would have traded money for time with my kids. I would have missed out on all the firsts in their life - first step, first word, first taste of green beans and the hilarious face that followed. I wouldn't have been the one to teach them to read. To watch the delight and joy on their face as they finally grasp a math concept. I wouldn't be the one to answer their questions all-day-long.

But also, from that salary would come greater taxes, and all the other expenses mentioned above that come with holding down a job in corporate America. And in reality, if had I continued to work, we likely would have managed to increase our lifestyle to match the

First time I've seen the top of my car in over 3 months!

income -- so whatever money was left after taxes and expenses, we would likely have spent it as quickly as I made it.

Instead, I sit here today with not even a fraction of that amount to my name. But I have my kids. I have a marriage that failed when my husband walked out - I'm not about to lose my children too. I'm not about to trade convenience or even the expectations of others by being the next one to abandon them as I pursue a career.

The choice to make my children my top earthly priority does not mean I have abandoned aspirations but it does mean I pursue them differently.

I first strive after Christ. Then I am a mother to these children. Thirdly, I am now unfortunately in the position of not only being mother but also having to be provider and I trust that in God's timing He will bring to fruition various projects and pursuits that I am capable of completing. Ultimately whether I work for another company or I work for myself it is the LORD who is my provider. So I will continue to trust HIM for provision as I pursue my calling at home.

In the meantime, I have heartfelt thanks to each and every family in the network that opened their home to my children and me, complete strangers yet family. None knew our story when they said yes and very few knew by the time we left their home, but it is to each of you that I dedicate this book.

Where was God?

A common question to a story like ours is "Where was God?"

"Where was God when all this was happening to you?"

"Why didn't God spare you/your children from this hardship?"

Or said another way, "If God is good, why did He allow this bad thing to happen to you?"

There are three ways this question is asked; each one is revealing.

"Where was *your* God?" said in a sarcastic manner will likely come from non-Christians. It is certainly the tone I would have asked the question in when I was an unbeliever.

It's as much a statement as it is a question. It is stated with the assumption that God isn't actually real – clearly He isn't real because if the Christian God was real this wouldn't have happened. It is stated as a way to mock the Christian faith.

The heart of this question was stated in this very tone by one of my critics at the onset of our trip. "Where is this God you keep saying will provide for you?"

The one speaking this thought she won the argument. Debate over.

Another way this question is asked is in anger; often from Christians who have a misunderstanding of the will and purposes of the Lord. This question is asked with the false assumption that a trial of this magnitude should never happen to "good people." The belief that a faithful, kind, good God would never allow such hardship to come to one of His children.

The third way the question is asked is in brokenness and despair. Like many of the Psalms, this person cries out, "Where was God?" wanting to know what could possibly be the purpose of such a hard trial. This person doesn't lack faith in God's goodness but lacks understanding.

So let me attempt to answer the question of where was God.

He was with us, every moment of every day. He was leading and guiding us. He was answering prayer – both mine and that of friends from "back home" asking the Lord to be our provider.

"Yeah, but you guys were homeless. How did God provide?"

He provided every second of everyday. He provided food each and every day. He provided places to stay. He provided a car that drove a ridiculous amount of miles without breaking down.

He provided a family to fix our flat tire.

He provided safety over all 10,974 miles from the myriad of dangers for anyone, let alone a single woman with four children.

He provided the strength to get up each day and care for my children. The strength to continue on when everything within me wanted to give up.

So, is this God that I worship some kind of masochistic bully that gains joy in watching one of His followers in such despair?

No. He is a loving, perfect Father who is willing to bring hardship in my life for my good.

Yes, you read that right. No, it's not a typo. For my good.

Am I angry at God for any of this? For my husband leaving? For being displaced 4 times in 3 years? For being homeless for over 3 months, being forced to travel the country aimlessly? No, I am grateful.

I am grateful that the Lord loves me enough to change me. I am grateful that He has taken me on a journey that required every ounce of my being to trust and rely on Him and Him alone. A journey that has brought my prayer life to a level that would otherwise be un-reachable. A journey that has given both my children and me a glimpse into authentic, Christian love and hospitality.

I am grateful that He has revealed to me various secret idols of my heart. Pride. Self righteousness. Lack of faith.

To the skeptic asking with malice, "Where was your God" I say this:

if you want to use my experience as a reason to justify your unbelief, it won't work. You see trials as evidence of no God. I see trials as evidence for my God. At the end of the day you are left with the same question; what will you do when you face this God you fight against? (Read Appendix B for more on this).

To the Christian who is angry, may I appeal to you briefly? If you are angry because you see the evils of the world, even the evils that have touched your life and cry "Foul! No fair!" May I encourage you to go back to the gospel. You and I have no place to be angry with God. He is GOD and can do whatever He please. And we are not good people to whom bad things happen. We are bad people deserving of the wrath of God. But God, in His great mercy has offered us eternal life through repentance and faith. And in this life, He pours out his kindness on us in everyday graces.

That does not mean we won't have struggles in this life. It actually means the opposite. The Bible promises us tribulations (Acts 14:22, 1Peter 1:6). We can be sure that this Christian life will have many trials. Those trials, however, aren't accidents that catch God by surprise. Instead, they come from His very hand – His sovereign hand -- in order to fulfill Romans 8:28. He will work those trials for good in your life, according to His purpose. And the ultimate purpose is to make you like His Son; to grow you in love, joy, peace, patience, goodness, kindness, faithfulness, gentleness and self-control. Does that sound familiar?

One of the many things I have learned over the last three years is that my trial isn't just about me. God is also working in the lives of others. Possibly bringing unbelievers to faith. Certainly giving believers an opportunity to minister to a sister in need. Glorifying Himself as both believers and unbelievers see my needs being met and a strength being given, enabling me to press on.

I am not the center of God's plan. I am merely a part of His plan and He is using my life to work out His greater purposes, and I am okay with that. Actually, I am thrilled with that because I can entrust every aspect of my life to the only One who knows all things, can do all things and is for my good, a greater and eternal good.

But in the midst of the trial He does have specific purposes for me.

He is making me more like His Son. Making me more compassionate towards others. More patient towards my children. More reliant upon HIM for ALL THINGS. More grateful for blessings. More sensitive about sin in my life. More humble, enabling me to more quickly repent when I sin…usually.

If you are a child of God, your current trial is not a punishment (Romans 8:1), nor has He forgotten about you. No, this trial is His MERCY on your life. It's a *mercy*. It is His means to sanctify you. Stop fighting it and embrace it. Ask Him, "Lord, what do you want me to learn from this?" I'm serious. Stop reading right now and ask Him. I promise you there is at least one lesson that He has for you.

To those that are simply hurting, feeling crushed under the weight of your trial, please know that God is with you. There is a popular saying; "God will never give you more than you can handle." This is false. It's not scripture.

God will *absolutely* give you more than you can handle so that you *must* turn to Him for the strength to persevere.

Paul David Tripp has said, "God will take you where you haven't intended to go in order to produce in you what you could not achieve on your own." I had that quote on an index card in our old apartment, until we were evicted. It was tucked in my Bible for a time as we were between apartments for 8 weeks. It was then on the refrigerator in our new apartment until we left for our homeless trek 6 months ago. It is a quote I read daily. Sometimes hourly if the day is particularly hard. It is 100% true and 100% hard to swallow.

God has indeed taken me where I NEVER intended to go and through that He has produced in me things I could NEVER have achieved on my own. And for all of that I can say with a clear conscience, "Lord, thank You for every aspect of this trial. Please don't ever repeat it, but thank You."

Your trial may have nothing to do with your own sin. It may have been thrust upon you. Maybe the unexpected death of a spouse or a child. Maybe illness or injury, and you are thinking, "I didn't do anything to deserve this." But you forget, this trial isn't a punishment, it's a mercy. It isn't getting in the way of God's plan for your life, it IS God's plan for your life because *through* this trial He is using it as His tool for your sanctification.

But maybe your sin is involved in your circumstance. You may have sinned and that sin is part and parcel a cause of your current trial.

My trial began with a relationship problem; a spouse that eventually left and pursued divorce. No matter how much he is at fault, the reality is that there are always 2 sinners in every conflict. While it was his sins that ultimately were the topic of disagreement and it was his choice to leave, there are still many things I'd do differently if given the chance. Things I wish I hadn't said and hadn't done. Responses I wish were more representative of the Gospel of grace, not the wrath of Melissa. But I cannot undo any of that.

What I can do and have done is repent and seek forgiveness first from the God who has already shown His mercy upon the cross and then from the very one responsible for much of the pain and hurt I have felt for many years. Humbling? Yes! But there is no price too great for a clear conscience before the Lord!

Understand this; the Lord is using even your sin to bring about your sanctification. God uses sin sinlessly, as radio host and author Todd Friel often says.

You can ruin yourself by over analyzing every misstep, every word spoken, and every detail of your circumstance to figure out what you could have done differently. I know! I've spent a decent amount of time doing just that to try to figure out where I went wrong and what I could have done to prevent my husband from leaving.

But hear me, even if your sin has brought upon your current trial, God was sovereign over it all; even over your sin.

He wasn't surprised by your sin and had to come up with plan B. His plan wasn't thrown off and now has to scramble to recover. The Lord allowed your sin to bring you to where you are today to do a work in you that could not have otherwise been done.

Read that again.

The Lord allowed your sin —
to bring you to where you are today—
to do a work in you—
that could not have otherwise been done.

That puts a different spin on it, doesn't it?

What that doesn't do is take away the pain. It doesn't magically remove the trial. But it does give you a different perspective on it.

Now pour into God's Word, seek Him in prayer and wait upon Him to move. Remember, He will never leave you nor forsake you." (Deuteronomy 31:6)

Appendix B

What Must I Do to be Saved?

I am a Christian. That is probably rather evident if you have read through this book. I don't apologize for my faith and I don't edit it out.

A childhood friend, upon hearing a very condensed version of what you just read said, "I'm amazed at your strength." I told her it's not my strength. If it were solely my strength I would have crumbled long ago. It is Christ that has given me the strength for every aspect of my journey, and every aspect of my life.

To many people Jesus Christ is a nice idea. They are "glad it works for me," but dismiss Him as simply a good teacher. Does that maybe describe you?

Others might agree to every aspect of the Christian message. Jesus was born of a virgin. He lived a perfect life. He died on the cross was buried and rose on the third day. He is the Savior. But there is a disconnect. What they say with their mouth does not seem to be believed with their heart because there is no evidence of a heart change, which the Bible makes clear will happen when a person truly repents of their sins and places their faith in Christ.

Still others look at Jesus as a Santa Claus story. It's a good story and fun to tell the kids, but it's not really true, and doesn't really matter, we're all going to heaven anyway.

The problem with each of these views is that they are wrong and the consequence for being wrong is deadly.

I know, I know, I can't tell people they are wrong these days. After all, truth is relative, right? We can all have our own personal beliefs, and that's cool, as long as I don't cross the politically correct line and state that someone else's "truth" isn't actually true. It's like we'd all rather live in a fantasy world than have the hard conversation and get down to the facts.

Before I became a Christian, I was a college kid trying to figure out life. For a season I looked into Scientology. They were nice people and it kind of, maybe made sense. But there were definitely some things that didn't seem right. I remember telling my roommate at the time, "I'd rather live in reality and be miserable than live in some fantasy world and be happy."

Thankfully it wasn't one or the other. When God found me and made me His I learned that I could both live in reality and be happy.

So what about you? Do you want to continue to pretend that the conflicting world views can ALL be right, or are you willing to take a few minutes, put on your thinking cap and walk down logic road with me?

Let's start with this. If nothing else, even if you still reject Christ, please be willing to admit this before you close this book or power off your kindle: WE CANNOT ALL BE RIGHT.

There are either many gods, one God or no gods. It's not a choose-your-own-adventure. Each option is mutually exclusive. Either there are many gods, ala Hinduism, or there are not. But Hinduism and Christianity cannot both be right. Logic tells us that TRUTH is narrowly defined. It is one or the other. And since both cannot be right, at least one of them is wrong. And if one of them is wrong, then it is important to know which is right. Right?

To set the record straight, there is only one God.

Are you still objecting?

2+2=4

Always

And Forever

2+2 will never equal 0, or 10000, or 50.

Your answer to 2+2 will either be correct or incorrect. If you write 4 then you are correct. Anything other than 4 is incorrect. And to say, "It doesn't matter. Everyone can have their own opinion" just doesn't make sense.

The same is true when we talk about eternity. Religions conflict. Christianity conflicts with every other religion out there, so Christianity is either true or it's not true. And which one it is matters a great deal. IF it is **true** and you reject it, eternity will not be pleasant.

So what exactly does Christianity claim? Good question. As a college freshman, I thought I knew what Christianity claimed because I grew up "in church." It wasn't until my senior year that I realized my understanding of Christianity was so very wrong.

Up to that point I always considered myself to be a pretty good person. I had long looked at my peers to gauge my goodness and when I saw the drunkenness and the promiscuity that was common I concluded that I was ahead of the curve.

But when I was confronted by what I heard from a preacher from New Zealand my self-righteousness came crumbling down. Ray Comfort used the Bible to show me that my self-proclaimed goodness was misplaced. I considered myself good because I had created my own standard – a standard that ignored my misgivings. But goodness isn't measured by my standard, it's measured by God's.

When Ray asked the following questions I felt like he was talking directly to me through my computer speakers as I sat in my dorm room.

"Have you ever told a lie?

"Have you ever stolen anything, *regardless* of its value?"

"Have you ever looked at another person with lust? God's sees that as adultery"

"Have you even been angry with someone and hated them? God says that is murder in the heart."

Looks like I wasn't so good after all.

After my self-righteousness was thoroughly destroyed I heard for the first time the Christian explanation for Jesus' death on the cross.

I grew up in a Lutheran church and heard often that Jesus died, He died for us. But that never made any sense. No one ever connected the dots for me. No one ever explained what sin was or that I was sinful. I was a good person, so why did I need some guy to die?

But once I understood that I was not good, I was wretched actually, then finally the death of Christ made sense.

You see, I am utterly sinFUL; Jesus was sinLESS.

I deserve to be punished for my crimes against God; Jesus deserves only good things.

Yet instead of punishing me, Jesus chose to be punished FOR me. The punishment I deserve was placed on Jesus Christ. Now God has granted me the gift of a repentant heart toward Him and faith towards the promises in Jesus. He has forgiven all of my sins because Someone else took my punishment.

It's a simple message and a simple truth. What will you do with it?

Had We Not Traveled

I took some time shortly after arriving at the bus to catalog our trip and to recall the many experiences that would have never occurred had we not traveled. Four years ago I never would have predicted the life we are currently living. I certainly never would have planned it this way and would never have anticipated it. But I can say in all honesty that I am thankful. I am thankful for being homeless. I am thankful for having to travel around the country because we had nowhere to live. I am thankful we left behind 90+% of our belongings.

Had we not been homeless we never would have traveled.

Had we not traveled we would not have seen the gorgeous waterfalls at Yosemite National Park.

We would not have sledded down the dunes at White Sands in New Mexico.

We would never have stood in awe as we looked up at Mount Rushmore.

We would never have traveled up the St. Louis Arch.

Had we not traveled we never would have met all of the amazing families that have hosted us, a number of whom have turned into wonderful friends.

I would not have learned to sew a dress.

My kids would not have milked a cow and ridden a horse.

My girls would not have received numerous piano lessons and still would not know how to knit or crochet.

I never would have received encouragment from folks who have endured trials of different sorts in their own lives.

I never would have met a fellow single mom who is determined to raise her children in the fear and admonition of the Lord despite external circumstances.

Had we not traveled I would never have met Trina Holden and this book you are reading would not exist.

Had we not left most of our belongings behind in NY I would never have felt the freedom of traveling with everything I own in a way that makes my belongings a blessing not a burden.

We never would have settled where we are now, in small town Alabama and been introduced to the wonderful folks of Redeemer Church.

My son would not have gone camping for the first time with a weekend full of "guy" activities because we would not have met Jeremy Holden, who offered to take him to our church's men's retreat.

The list goes on and will continue to go on as quickly as life goes on.

This is not the first time I have looked at dismal circumstances and have rejoiced. No, I'm not masochistic. It's just that I cling to the truth found in Romans 8:28 - whether I can see the good in that moment or not. I know for a fact that the hardships we have faced have been from the benevolent hand of my Lord, for my good and ultimately for His own glory. If He is taking me through a hardship it is to refine me and make me more like His Son. To wean me away from my idols. To reveal hidden sins in my heart. To make me more patient. More compassionate to others facing trials. To bring me to my knees in a way that prosperity cannot. To remind me that He alone is my provider, my strong tower, my faithful husband.

I am a different person today because of all that we have endured. And while I would never have chosen this and have no desire to repeat any of it, I am eternally grateful that my Father loved me enough to give me what I NEED and not what I WANT. I did not want any of this hardship, but I needed it -- to become the person He wanted me to be.

To rephrase Paul Tripp's quote:

"God [has taken me] where [I hadn't] intended to go in order to produce in [me] what [I] could not achieve on [my] own."

Acknowledgements

I am super excited to write this section because it gives me a chance to publicly declare my immense appreciation for all of you wonderful people who have worked in my life far beyond what you can know. I am completely indebted to the **A Candle in the Window** network that was God's hands and feet over our 3 months of travel. **Allison Crawford** who is in and under each page of this book and every day of our travels. AdvoCare was not about creating my Plan B– it was about meeting you. You kept me moving forward (and still do) with your encouragements and (as needed) rebukes. I value your friendship more than you know! **Jeremy and Trina Holden**, without whom this book would not exist and this story would not have a happy ending. Thank you for your friendship. Thank you for the encouragement to write this story. Thank you for your bus. Thank you for being a wonderful example of Christian hospitality. **Pastor Ryan Limbaugh** and **Reedemer Church of Oxford, AL**. We have found our church home and could not be any more thrilled to sit under your teaching and leadership. To my dear friend **Rebekah**, for your editing help, for you listening ear, for your dedication to prayer. To **Jamie Limbaugh** – your friendship is truly refreshing. I don't know that you'll ever get done reading the story to see your name here, but it's here nonetheless. Thank you for being you and for intersecting with my life. The **Ben Brown** and **Chris Hyche** for helping me edit this story. And to my Lord Jesus Christ – may you use this story for Your glory; whatever that looks like. Take my life and let it be all for you and for your glory. Use my ransomed life in any way you choose.

About the Author:

Melissa is a graduate of the Wharton School of the University of Pennsylvania. After a brief stint in the corporate world where fortune was within her reach, she came home to be a wife, mother, and homemaker. Life didn't quite go as planned and the fairy tale ended leaving her a single mom of four kids - all under the age of 8. Rather than giving up or giving in, she dug in her heels and remained true to her convictions. An epic road trip later she and her children went from being homeless vagabonds to once again finding roots and community. Melissa homeschools her children, is currently learning Latin along side them, and is diving back into the world of road races.

Journeytosomewherestory.com

Melissaamaya.com

Made in the USA
Middletown, DE
11 October 2016